HITLER'S HOUSEWIVES

In memory of Cy Garrett – 24 August 1976 to 15 June 2016 – and his father Dave Garrett – 25 August 1952 to 2 April 2018. Family lives in the heart forever. You both left much too soon. Yet we will remember you both with great love and affection always. I feel honoured to have been able to call you family however brief that time may have been.

HITLER'S HOUSEWIVES

German Women on the Home Front

TIM HEATH

PEN & SWORD **HISTORY**

AN IMPRINT OF PEN & SWORD BOOKS LTD.
YORKSHIRE - PHILADELPHIA

First published in Great Britain in 2020 by
PEN AND SWORD HISTORY
An imprint of
Pen & Sword Books Ltd
Yorkshire – Philadelphia

ISBN 978 1 52674 807 2

Typeset in Times New Roman 11.5/14 by
Aura Technology and Software Services, India.
Printed and bound in the UK by TJ International

Pen & Sword Books Limited incorporates the imprints of Atlas, Archaeology,
Aviation, Discovery, Family History, Fiction, History, Maritime, Military, Military
Classics, Politics, Select, Transport, True Crime, Air World, Frontline Publishing,
Leo Cooper, Remember When, Seaforth Publishing, The Praetorian Press,
Wharncliffe Local History, Wharncliffe Transport, Wharncliffe True Crime and
White Owl.

For a complete list of Pen & Sword titles please contact
PEN & SWORD BOOKS LIMITED
47 Church Street, Barnsley, South Yorkshire, S70 2AS, England
E-mail: enquiries@pen-and-sword.co.uk
Website: www.pen-and-sword.co.uk

Or

PEN AND SWORD BOOKS
1950 Lawrence Rd, Havertown, PA 19083, USA
E-mail: Uspen-and-sword@casematepublishers.com
Website: www.penandswordbooks.com

Contents

Introduction

The meteoric rise of Adolf Hitler and the Nazi Party cowed the masses into a sense of false utopia. With an economy steadily geared towards war throughout the 1930s, by 1938 the scourge of unemployment in Germany had all but been eradicated. Hitler believed that Germany had been a nation subjugated to materialism and that prosperity could only ever be gained through struggle and war. In the relatively brief period of its existence, Nazi Germany had been devoid of any clear economic objective, yet the women of Germany played a crucial role in Hitler's rise to power. It has been suggested that, during Hitler's 1932 election campaign, over half of those who voted for him were women. They had witnessed the anarchy of the post-war years in Germany and experienced the economic and social privations that resulted from an Allied-brokered peace. The women of Germany had also witnessed first-hand the chaos brought about by rival gangs brawling on their streets, the result of over forty different political factions all vying for power in this blighted land. Unemployment had been the greatest single threat to the stability of family life in Germany at that time. The depression years brought about not only severe social hardships of every conceivable kind but also a high mortality rate amongst the country's young. In a place where even the most basic of foodstuffs such as a loaf of bread became luxury items, malnutrition and disease soon took hold; children were usually the first to perish under such conditions. It was not unusual during those years of hardship for families to lose four out of six children.

When Hitler came to power there was at last a ray of hope in what appeared an impenetrable darkness; that this man of the people would restore not only political stability to the country but also prosperity to its people. As reforms were set in place, Hitler encouraged women to step aside from their jobs and allow men to take their places. Initially the theory worked and Germany's female population followed their leader's instructions. Their duties as guardians of the home were to be the very foundation for a future 'Thousand-Year Reich'. Germany's women readily accepted this as recompense for Germany's journey back to greatness, though not all embraced the principle of living in a society where two distinct worlds existed: that of men and that of women. With the outbreak of the Second World War, however, Germany's women would soon find themselves on the front line. As fathers, sons, brothers and boyfriends went off to war women faced the unique challenges that the home front would present. Divided by their roles as mothers and housewives, they accepted the ambiguities of their leaders.

The home front is a crucial factor for any nation during times of protracted war. The home front is where society itself becomes mobilised towards the goal of victory. Although the leadership of Nazi Germany understood the lessons learned from the First World War, during the Second World War the Nazi home front was somewhat slow in mobilising. The main reasons for this were twofold. The first point to consider is that during the early phase of the Second World War America had yet to enter hostilities alongside Britain and France. Germany had yet to experience the mass air raids on her cities and industrial bases. Therefore, Germany's infrastructure was, at this early stage, largely unaffected. Secondly, it was not until 1941 – after the invasion of Russia – that Germany would be faced with the reality of fighting a war on two fronts. America's entry into the Second World War, following the Japanese attack on US Naval forces at Pearl Harbor, sealed Germany's fate. From 1941 the country would be locked in a fight for survival that it could not possibly win. The realisation that victory would be neither quick (as Hitler had hoped) nor without huge cost in lives meant that Germany's women would soon form a significant part of the war effort.

As the war progressed manpower became a problem. As more and more men were required on the battlefront it would be the women of Germany who would have to take their places in every sphere of life. Effective management of the home front often has a huge influence upon the outcome of any war. Perhaps the best examples of this would be that of Britain and America. In Germany's case all the efforts, no matter how great they may have seemed at the time, only served to prolong the inevitable outcome. The desperate situation faced by the country, particularly through the mid-war years, should have been warning enough as to the outcome of a war that Germany had started. Women rose bravely to every challenge they faced, despite steadily increasing privations, as well as the death and destruction that surrounded them. They had made the transition from housewives and as bearers of children to defenders of the Third Reich and, convinced through indoctrination and propaganda, that theirs was a divine task, they followed the leadership into the flames of war. Even the young girls of the *Jungmadelbund* (Young Maidens League) and *Bund Deutscher Madel* (League of German Maidens) could not escape the mobilisation of the home front. As the war against Germany neared its climax in 1945, every possible resource had been exploited. When the end came it was neither merciful nor pleasant.

Ultimately Hitler's housewives experienced mixed fortunes throughout the years of the Second World War: there were those whose loved ones went off to war never to return; those who lost children not only to the influences of the Hitler Youth but the Allied bombing; those who sought comfort within the arms of other young men; and those who would serve above and beyond the call of duty on the German home front. Their stories form intimate and intricately woven tales of life, love, joy, fear and death. *Hitler's Housewives: German Women on the Home Front 1939-1945* is not only an essential document towards a better understanding of one of the twentieth century's greatest tragedies but also, and for the first time, tells the story of the role played by Germany's women on the home front in their own words.

'There was a sense of relief that the war was now finally over, yet there was this darkness within our souls that I could never imagine leaving any of us who had experienced it.'

Helga Koerg, Kassel, Germany,1996.

Chapter 1

A New Euphoria

'So, don't you blame us for the violence on our streets, you can blame the government, blame the state police'.

Helena Marschmann had grown up in a working-class family in the German city of Kassel, in the Hesse region of west-central Germany. As a teenager, she was described as a pretty girl, though shy and somewhat awkward. Many of the local boys had expressed an interest in her yet many of them had failed to impress her. Her upbringing had been a strict one, though no more strict than any other girl of her community. Helena had a brother, three years her senior, named Peter. By the age of twenty-four she was a mother of three young girls. Her husband, Reinhard Koerg, worked at a pharmacy in the city. The two had known each another from their years at the same school. It seemed Reinhard was the only boy who could have ignited the fire within a heart described by many as being quite cold. Both had experienced the remarkable events that had led to Adolf Hitler's Nazi Party being swept to power, but were unconcerned initially. They were both in employment enjoying the privacy of their small, yet adequate city home. Helena and Reinhard were fortunate as many young couples were forced to live with in-laws during the early phase of marriage. As a couple able to enjoy such simple pleasures, they believed the Nazi Party was delivering on its promises to the German people. Helena believed that the events of 1 September 1939 were the beginnings of something very special for all Germans of true German blood. She began writing a very detailed journal as she, like many others, could not foresee the disaster that was to come. Helena reflected upon that fateful day, Friday, 1 September 1939:

> The bell of the small Junghans alarm clock rings at 6.00am for the second time this morning. Its chimes pierce the

silence of early morning at 5.00am when Reinhard had to be roused for work. I rise stiffly from the warmth of the bed and sit on the edge stretching my legs out. My stomach is gnarled with menstruation pains. How I could just go back to sleep but I can't. The cool Autumnal air in the room has the embrace of a ghost as I try to wake up fully. The girls are fast asleep in the next room. I will leave them there for a few more minutes until I am washed and dressed. I splash the cold water over my face and eyes and stare at myself momentarily in Reinhard's small shaving mirror. I think to myself "You look a mess brush your hair!" I dry myself off, dress and brush my hair. I put some water on to boil for coffee. Like most modern girls today my body appears to function much better after two cups of hot, black coffee. I drink my coffee standing in the doorway of the girl's bedroom.

Our three girls, Gertrud, Helga and Ilsa, look so peaceful as they sleep in their warm beds. I put my coffee down and gently rouse them by caressing their little heads. They moan and groan and their little eyes open as if a blinding light is being shone into their faces. I say to them "come on you three little sleepy heads school will not wait for you." They each take it in turns to run downstairs to the outside toilet in the back yard. Gertrud, the eldest, makes it to the toilet first while the others wait in the kitchen impatiently for her to finish. They quarrel amongst themselves and I have to remind them to hurry along. They run back upstairs complaining about the cold. I help them to dress and do their hair ready for school. The time goes nowhere, soon we are leaving the house to make the short journey to school. We almost run in the vain hope we will avoid being late. Vehicles drive precariously close to the kerbs in the town. The girls scream as a car drives through the gutters sending a small wave of putrid water towards them. I shout at the drivers "You idiots! Can't you see where you are going?" They can't hear me so it makes little difference.

In the town the newspaper vendors are waving their wares to the passing public. Many are talking excitedly about the invasion of Poland, which has been in progress since the early hours of this morning. The headlines of the newspapers catch the eyes of passers-by. The headlines address the tensions between Britain, France and Germany. It does not worry me at all and I think nothing of it all. We will listen to the radio to find out what it is all about. How could any country threaten our mighty Germany, maybe a foolhardy one? If we are to be at war then it probably will not last long. Our army and Luftwaffe are the most powerful forces in the world. Maybe this time next year we will all be holidaying in Paris or on an English beach and looking across the Channel towards home reviewing a great victory.

I go into my favourite coffee house where yet another hot coffee revives me to the point where I feel ready to go to work. Coffee always tastes better when someone else has made it for you. The atmosphere of the coffee shop is one of excitement as people discuss the news of Poland. I arrive at the bakery shop two minutes late. I throw my coat over the hanger and put on an apron. Herr Fauschner complains that the pastries I was meant to prepare are still not ready. He says, "How can I run a business like this if everyone was just two minutes late where would we all be?" I smile and kiss him on the cheek. He says that I am lucky I am one of his favourite employees. The pastries, strudels, cakes and breads are soon coming out of the old stone oven in quick succession.

Helena marvels at the dexterity of Herr Fauschner's heavily knotted fingers as he rolls small pieces of pastry into sweet delights, ready for baking. Compared to hers, his fingers resemble the broken twigs from an old oak tree. His ageing features give him an almost gerbil-like facial appearance. Helena thought this often and she had to stifle a smile each time the thought crossed her mind. The old man was a veteran of the 1914-1918 Great War yet he would never talk of his experiences. He forbade any talk of war in his presence. A gentleman of the old school, he understood that war in any form was the harbinger of misery.

The shelves in the shop are soon full and people are waiting outside the door. When the door is opened they converge like a herd of cattle, all excitedly discussing the latest topic of conversation. Helena continues:

> The news of the invasion of Poland is met with mixed reactions. The older people are not enthusiastic about it all, reminding those that are about what occurred in 1918 and beyond. "1918 shall never happen again," we younger ones say. "We will all have to die before we allow it." By lunchtime the shelves of the shop are virtually empty. I will have to go to get the girls from school. I grab my coat from the hanger and take a small loaf of brown rye bread from the shelf. I am allowed a loaf per day for free as I work there. I take a pastry each for the girls tell everyone I will see them in the morning. Herr Fauschner shouts for me not to be late in the morning. He laughs as he says this as I disappear out onto the busy street outside. My stomach still hurts but I still have lots to do. I collect the girls from school and we head off home. When we arrive home the girls help me to get the fire going. They then help me to prepare the evening meal. With the food prepared I am able to sit down for an hour to help the girls with their school chores before Reinhard arrives home.
>
> When Reinhard walks through the front door dinner is placed on the table. He sits before his meal, insisting the radio is switched on to catch the latest news. The girls, oblivious to all of the excitement, eat their food as innocently as any child would while we discuss the day's events. Reinhard is not concerned about the invasion of Poland. "It is nothing to worry about. Should the English and French intervene and declare war against us it is still nothing," he says as he eats his food. "England is an Empire of course but France is of no concern. France will be defeated relatively easily should war come between our countries." I ask the typical questions a young woman might ask, even though I know nothing about the conduct of wars or their intricate tactical matters. I know that wars cost lives and some of the older people do not want war in Germany.

My mother and father will not be happy about this news. My father used to say that Hitler was trouble, even before he became our leader. Father was not happy about our girls having to join the *Jungvolk* organisation. He insists that children should be allowed to be children and that politics should not form a part of their childhood. My father and I could argue over Reich policy all day sometimes. The fact we are a nation prepared to go to war again is both frightening and exciting at the same time. My brother is in military training with the Luftwaffe and it will be interesting to see what he says about all of this when he visits with mother, father and grandfather on Sunday. Does he know things that we don't? Reinhard insists the war should not be discussed by women. He is of the opinion that the war will be fought and won by the men of Germany.

After our meal we all go out for a short walk. There is a strange atmosphere amongst the populace. The girls run ahead of us, oblivious to the adult world and its problems which surround them. Yet I know the *Jungvolk* has already convinced them of who the bogeymen are within our society. They don't fully understand it all but neither do I in some ways. I feel slightly uneasy as we walk back home from the small wooded park. For a short time everyday problems are left behind. You feed the birds; watch the animals scurry about and admire the views, trees and water. It's like the world stands still for that particular moment. I stroll back with Reinhard and we walk arm in arm. The girls chase each other playing cats and dogs, their plaited hair flails about as they run. It makes me smile as they bring back fond memories of my own youth. When we arrive home the girls are told to get ready for bed and I come and read them a story to help send them towards pleasant dreams. Ilsa, our youngest daughter, who is six years of age, asks me, "Mummy, what does the war mean? Is it bad?" The Nazis have been going on about war for years in our schools. They believe even the young should be prepared for war and struggle. What can I say to her other than "Do not trouble your little head with such things."

It is never a good idea to criticise the policies implemented by our leadership. Our role is to obey and follow whatever happens. Anyone who fails to adhere to policy will go the way of the Jew that is for sure. We don't know where they [the Jews] have all gone from around here but they have all gone. Even the good old Dr Messner has disappeared. I know he was a Jew but he was a great doctor. I can only imagine the Jews from around here have been ejected from our country, fled or maybe even killed. I really don't know and I don't want to think about it. Nobody dares to ask questions here in our town. We have a new Dr Bloehm who now sees us and our girls if they need to see a doctor. Bloehm has a painting of Hitler hanging in his surgery room and a large party flag hangs behind his desk. Bloehm is a stern character and rarely smiles. He is more like a schoolteacher with a head of stone than a doctor. Whenever I see him he reminds me to look after my girls as they are the focus of Germany's future. The permeation of politics into everyday life can be boring but it's there to remind us and not to allow us to forget.

Sunday, 3 September began as many other Sundays in Germany. Traditionally it was a day where families would go to church, have lunch together, and share part of the evening quietly discussing events over a tea of sandwiches. The news that Britain had made its declaration of war against Germany for its invasion of Poland failed to affect the appetites of the Koerg family at breakfast. Helena recalled:

Our neighbour has just run round in an excited state of panic. He says, "Britain and France have declared war against us; we are now at war with the English and French again." I was washing up the breakfast things when he came running around. He would always cut through the vegetable patch which he used as a short cut. The poor, excited fellow almost fell over in his haste. Reinhard heard the commotion and turned on the radio to find out if it was true. Sure enough, the news is true; we are now at war with England and France. For a moment there is silence, apart from our two youngest girls who are playing at the kitchen table with their dolls. Reinhard breaks the silence with the words "It will all be alright it is nothing for any of us to be worried about".

When my mother, father and brother arrive for dinner the topic collapses into heated debate and discussion. My grandfather thinks it's dreadful news and he is angry, saying, "Hitler must be bereft of sanity. How could he get us into another war?" My father on the other hand expresses cautious optimism at the news. He remarks, "If all of this goes to plan Germany will become the greatest nation on earth. We can and will decisively defeat the French, then the door will be kicked down to the British Empire and that would make us very strong indeed." I ask my brother Peter for his military perspective. After all, he should know should he not? He says bluntly, "From our military perspective the consensus of opinion is that should Britain and France intervene, as we guessed they would, they can be defeated by way of a concentrated air campaign against their airfields in the south of England. In my opinion it is perfectly feasible and victory of sorts could be achievable within weeks. The French will not be able to stand up to our Blitzkrieg. We will use troops, armour and aircraft as we have in Poland. France will fall quickly, I can tell you that." I ask him where he came by this information and he tells me, "We have been discussing this over the past few months. Of course, we have to deal with the French first. Conquer France and we have the stepping stone to our Führer's conquest of England. Our training is almost complete and soon we will be flying in direct support of our invading forces." There was silence again for a few minutes as I began to put the food onto plates. Everyone was sat around the table patiently waiting for their roasted pork meat and vegetables. As I dished out the food I thought of housewives back in England. Will they be doing the same as us here? Are they afraid of what is going to happen next? The French are just next door to us. They must be feeling very uneasy. There are so many questions at this time yet it is so exciting in the same instance.

As we eat dinner Peter is boastful again of the mighty Luftwaffe. He says, "The French are nothing more than a formality while the British do not possess as good an aerial bombing capability as ours. We have many bomber aircraft and our fighters are the best there are." I ask him, "Dear brother, do you not feel fear at the prospect of combat?" He replies, "Quite the contrary. No, I don't. Effective use of any combat aircraft lies in the courage and resourcefulness of its pilot. We have been trained well and we have the best equipment for the task ahead in the Messerschmitt Me 109." I remark at what a peculiar name that is for an aircraft. With his mouth full his reply is barely audible, "Yes, and it is the best fighter in the world in my own opinion." Grandfather listens yet says little. The expression on his face shows perfectly his mood regarding this matter. He turns to father and asks him, "And what of your opinion? How do you feel about your son going to war?" Father replies, "I am very proud of him and I am sure he will serve his country with the pride it deserves. I am not saying war is always right, but in this instance I believe that it is an unavoidable course of action for Germany."

The girls have cleared their plates and eagerly await their dessert of apple strudel, which is a traditional German fruit dessert. The apples have been stored in the shed and we should be able to enjoy them for some weeks. I clear the table of plates and portion the desserts for everyone. Mother has been very quiet throughout and I ask her if she is alright. She appears lost in thought and this is understandable. She flickers a smile and just remarks on what a superb dinner she has just eaten. It is clear she does not wish to discuss anything to do with war. Cream is poured onto the portions of strudel and everyone eats their dessert heartily. After dessert the girls ask for permission to go out and play with their friends. I tell them not to go far and to keep away from the nearby wood. I told them there are werewolves in those woods. When they asked me what a werewolf was I told them it is a man who may look like any other but can change into a ravenous, flesh-eating creature, half-man, half-wolf covered in black fur with long fangs and red eyes which can see in the dark. It was what my mother used to tell me to prevent me from going anywhere she did not want me going. I didn't want the girls going into the woods as there were vagrants from the city residing in there at times. I know the local boys go there and talk with them but I am not allowing my girls to do the same. The tale of werewolves works beautifully and the girls keep within sight of our home.

As the kitchen table is cleared Reinhard, mother, father, grandfather and Peter retire to the living room. We wish grandmother was still with us; how we miss her so. She had been gone one year and two months now, yet it seems a lifetime ago. I wash the crockery, pans and dishes and make drinks for us all. Grandfather is fast asleep in the chair. The old man reminds me so much of Fauschner at the bakery. A woman's work is never done though. No sooner has dinner been cleared I make some sandwiches and use some of the now cold meat from dinner with some home pickled vegetables for tea. Sunday is such a social occasion for us. The one day of the week where we all get together as a family is over so quickly. At tea time we listen to music on the radio. Sometimes Gertrud will play the piano for us. I watch her with so much admiration as her slender fingers tap the keys to make such sweet melodies. Every time Gertrud completes a piece there is a round of applause from us all. She stands and gives a bow and I marvel at not only how beautiful but how grown up our eldest daughter is. She will be ten in a few days' time. No doubt the war will be discussed in school tomorrow too. Gertrud will announce with some pride that her uncle is a fighter pilot who might possibly be fighting the English soon. Her friends and the other children in the class will be envious of her. Before mother, father, Peter and grandfather leave, Peter pats Gertrud on the head and tells her, "You will soon be joining the *Jungmadelbund* after your tenth birthday. You will learn all sorts of new things that will prepare you for the new Germany." Grandfather interrupts and remarks, "What? And fill her head full of rubbish. If you have any common sense you will keep that treasure of a girl far away as you can from the political filth that is the Hitler Youth." Peter laughs at him and I hear him say, "Oh, grandfather, come on now it's not that bad, and a girl needs to understand her place otherwise we would end up just as the racial sewers throughout Europe and beyond." Their argument continues as they walk out of the front door. We all exchange kisses and wave them off.

I then have to make sure the girls have a wash and put on their nightclothes ready for bed. Gertrud is happily doing this by herself while the other two wait patiently for her to finish. When they have put on their nightgowns I send them up to bed with the promise of a story. The volume of Grimms Tales is a well-worn childhood favourite that I have treasured over the years. Immersing myself in words of fantasy was my way of escaping the bullying I often experienced in my youth. I vow that anyone who bullies my girls will have to answer to me personally. When they are tucked up in bed I sit beside them and read them a story. They are fast asleep before the story even ends. I sit and watch them for a few minutes before leaving the room, closing the door behind me.

Reinhard is sleeping in the chair in the living room. The radio is on the news station. I turn it back to listen to music. I have heard enough politics and have had my fill of this new euphoria for one day. What will the old man Fauschner think of all this at work in the morning? I shake Reinhard by the shoulder to wake him up. I tell him, "Come on, let's go to bed for the night." He rises to his feet like a drunk so I grab his arm and help him up to bed. He wearily undresses then sits there watching me as I undress and brush my hair. Suddenly the fatigue of this day's excitement dissipates. He pulls me towards him and our bodies meet in a strong embrace. Tumbling into the cool, white sheets of the marital bed the sex is vigorous and urgent, if somewhat rough. By the time we have both climaxed we fall into an instant slumber in each other's arms. I wake in the early hours as the sweat has dried upon my body, releasing a chill. I get up, put on my nightdress and climb back into bed. I am soon fast asleep again yet before the alarm has even sounded in the early morning I wake up to find Reinhard caressing me between my legs. It is nice yet I want to sleep too. A woman has so many demands to fulfil. I sometimes wish I had been born a man instead of a woman.

Monday morning breaks with the usual busy routine of getting the girls up to get ready for school and me for work. I like the routine I have as it gives me a sense of freedom. It is pretty much just another Monday until the girls are collected from school. As we walk home, Gertrud, our eldest girl, talks of the *Jungmadelbund*. All her class friends have joined apart from her. Her teacher has questioned her as to why she has not joined yet. Admittedly it has been something I have been desperately trying to avoid for as long as possible. Gertrud is eager to join yet this has to be discussed with Reinhard when he arrives home from his work. When he arrives home we sit down for dinner, after which I send the girls out to their room while we talk. Reinhard explains he is happy for Gertrud to join but not for reasons of education or patriotism. He explains if she does not join we could be construed as being non-conformists to the wishes of our government. This government has served us well so far so why should we resist. "It won't do the girl any harm. On the contrary, it will be good for her," he says with a smile. I ask, "But what of the politics, what about that?" He sighs deeply and says, "Look this is the way it has to be. If it works out for the best for Germany, that educating our youth against the social pollution that minorities may be responsible for, then so be it. We have to get on. Besides, what other choices are there? I can go to the school and complain and risk upsetting the authorities, make things awkward for Gertrud and maybe even lose my job. I don't want to find out so let her join if it means keeping the peace. We will keep an eye on her don't you worry."

When Gertrud came out of school the next day with her sisters she was clutching some papers. The papers were forms which every parent both mother and father had to complete prior to their child joining the Hitler Youth. The questions were extensive and proof of ancestry going back two or three generations was required. For Reinhard and Helena this was not a problem. Their families had been born and raised in Germany and there was no question of any Jewish blood being present within the family lines. The questions addressed everything from birth dates and birthplaces of parents, grandparents and great grandparents, height, weight, colour of eyes and hair, occupations and dates of death where applicable. With two flourishes of an ink pen, Gertrud Koerg's *Jungmadelbund* membership application was complete. The form would be submitted to the authorities and a decision would then be based upon Gertrud's physical fitness.

As a ten-year-old, Gertrud Koerg was a lively, energetic child with no physical or mental impairment. She could run with the grace of a greyhound, climb trees faster than the boys and stand up for herself in an argument. The form submitted for her *Jungmadelbund* membership would surely be a mere formality. Gertrud recalled the medical examination that she had to undergo prior to her acceptance.

> They didn't want imbeciles as they called them. Anyone with a mental or physical impediment would be an embarrassment to the Hitler Youth. The Hitler Youth was all about showing off, prestige if you like. We were after all Hitler's youth and we represented the newly militarised Germany. My medical examination was like many carried out in school on children in those days. The Nazi doctors in charge of the Hitler Youth girls were quite invasive. They examined your eyes and eyesight, your hearing, your hair and scalp. Then they would get you to take off your clothes so you were just standing there in your knickers. I didn't mind this too much as both my examiners were women. I had to stand and raise my arms straight above my head while breathing in an out and they would listen to your lungs with one of those things doctors use [stethoscope]. They made you bend down and touch your toes then examined your legs and feet. It did not really last that long and the doctors were very pleased with me. They had looked at the family records from the information my parents provided and concluded

there were no what they termed as 'racial diseases' present in our family's history. I asked before I left if I was going to be able to join the girl's league and they said, "We are happy to tell you yes as we see no problems here. If you work very hard and promise to be a good German you will do well."

I left the examination room to go to my parents who were waiting outside. I was in an elated mood and was bouncing as they say. My father had to tell me to calm down. On my way home my parents were discussing the uniform. Mother said, "She doesn't really need to wear the uniform. She can wear her normal clothes." Father argued, "She will look nicer in uniform, besides I don't want my girl being the odd one out. The others will say her parents can't afford a uniform and things like that. No, she will have a uniform and I will see to it, and I will hear no more, Helena." There was a frosty silence the rest of the walk home through the town. I was happy in myself as I was just a young girl. I hadn't really envisaged what I had signed up for. Later on, I guess I understood why my poor mother had been a little reluctant.

My grandparents were not happy once they heard the news. Grandmother said, "Stigma is everything and it stays with one forever. What is Hitler doing with the youth of our country? For heaven's sake, why can't he leave them alone to do what children should be doing? I can't help but have concerns that he has ulterior motives with his Hitler children ideas. How much is this new euphoria going to cost us all?" Yes, my grandparents were wise old owls who had been in the forest long enough to smell the dangers which lurked there. I received my crisp, brand-new *Jungmadelbund* uniform of brown jacket, white blouse, black tie, dark skirt and leather ankle boots. I had a diamond-shaped badge which I pinned to the left breast of my jacket. When I tried it all on for the first time I could see the pride in my father's face. "Look at her. Does she not look beautiful," he said to mother. My father also ensured I had the correct sports clothing. It must have cost him a lot of money back then but he wanted me to have the full equipment. My grandparents looked slightly worried when they came over so that I could have my first portrait photograph in uniform taken. In fact, grandmother began to cry. She wiped the tears from her eyes and said something I would never forget. She said, "The girl looks more like a soldier. It is dreadful." She was almost bundled back into the house to avoid embarrassing father, who had an argument with my grandparents afterwards. I heard them shouting at one another but could not clearly hear what was being said. They both left our house and I didn't see them again for three months after the argument. It made me and my mother in particular very sad. It felt like our once happy family was slowly being torn apart by the events happening around us. Hitler had been in power six years but we were now at war. That changed a lot of things. War always changes things, but they do so for the worst."

Chapter 2

War? What War?

Kitka Obermann was a very striking looking German girl, born and raised in the city of Friedrichshafen, on Lake Constance in the extreme south of Germany. Whenever asked about her odd name she would explain that Kitka was the nickname her closest friends gave her growing up together in Friedrichshafen. Kitka's proper name was Katherina, yet she always preferred Kitka as it meant 'pure and clear' in Latin. She described her family as being quite wealthy. It is no surprise then that they were fully supportive of the National Socialists. Kitka's parents were very patriotic and held violently racist attitudes. Kitka had left full-time education at the tender age of fourteen. Her talents included being an excellent pianist and her mother had taught her both shorthand and typing. Kitka spent two years after leaving school helping her mother around their home. For a brief period she also became a housekeeper for another local wealthy family. After a few months she was given charge of looking after the family's four young children, a job she thoroughly enjoyed as she loved children. It was during her time there that she fell in love with a local man two years her senior. By the time she was seventeen, she was a married mother of one. Her husband's name was Joachim Obermann. Joachim worked as an engineering foreman at the Dornier aircraft plant. This was a prestigious and well-paid role for a man of his age.

Kitka's youth had not been without its troubles. She had inadvertently attracted the attention of the local Nazi authorities a few years previous by dating a local boy who was later found to have had Jewish ancestry. This episode caused her family much embarrassment and consternation. The boy Kitka had been dating was arrested and she never saw or heard from him again. Even his family vanished from their neighbourhood. Kitka recalls:

> I had no idea the boy had Jewish ancestry. Not that it really mattered to me. My parents were pretty vile people really.

A couple of days later, after the boy's arrest, my mother literally dragged me to the local doctor. She wanted to be sure that 'the Jew', as she referred to him, had not defiled her "stupid daughter". Even the doctor was cross with me. At my mother's insistence, I was made to take off my skirt and knickers while the doctor examined my vagina to determine whether or not I had been penetrated. I was crying as the whole thing was humiliating and painful. The fact that the doctor told my mother I was fine as my hymen appeared to be intact was no recompense. My mother thanked the doctor, grabbed me by the arm and frogmarched me back home. I spent hours in my room. My father had taken away all of my books apart from a bible. I wanted to escape this existence so badly and would lie awake, thinking on how I could do it. They tried relentlessly to impose their will upon me, along with their political allegiances.

When Poland was invaded by our army my parents were both ecstatic about it. They cheered and whooped for joy. When the English declared a state of war between our countries, they were still ecstatic. Both of them were of the opinion that Germany would smash the English this time. My father said, "France will be next. Our mighty forces will beat the French and anyone else who dares to challenge us. England will probably be invaded by next summer." When the men got together at work or in the beer halls they talked about these things. My father knew men who were serving in the *Wehrmacht*. These soldiers, having returned from Poland with their fantastic stories and showing off their Iron Cross medals, gave everyone confidence that this new war would go our way.

My parents had been obscenely strict with me and my two brothers. Father would tell my brothers, "As soon as you two are old enough you shall be soldiers." I couldn't be a soldier as I was a girl. I was told, "You shall sew the socks and sheets of soldiers. Women are the providers of comfort for the men of this nation who must stand up against our enemies in this world. One day we shall conquer the world." He used to make me sick with his bullying tirades.

Mother was just as bad, reminding us that she had endured pain and hardship to raise us and that we were all ungrateful to her suffering. As I grew older, they meddled further into every aspect of my life. I had my friends from school who I would talk to and in turn they would tell me things. We learned about the birds and the bees by telling one another things. Even bodily functions such as periods were not discussed, often until they occurred.

During the Second World War the city of Friedrichshafen would be subjected to extensive Allied bombing. The city was a hive of manufacturing in the German war effort. The Dornier aircraft works and Maybach tank engine factory were just two of the essential industries based in the city. Kitka continues:

Meeting Joachim was a turning point in my young life. Although we would later divorce, at the time we met it was something of a blessing. I did love him dearly and he loved me too. When I met him I was amazed that my family approved. Maybe it was because he was an engineer and also from a family not short of money. Joachim was the first boy that had ever made love to me. After our first time I became pregnant with my first child, a boy. My parents wanted me to marry as soon as possible. I was always their "stupid daughter". Joachim was respectful of them but he later admitted he did not particularly like them, especially my scornful mother, as he called her. I had hoped to work as a secretary in the Maybach offices. Maybach were building engines for our tanks but because I had discovered I was pregnant I cancelled my application and stayed in the small home we had bought with help from our parents. I say it was small yet it had five rooms in all. My parents' home had nine rooms in total, so I guess it was small by comparison.

Those early months of the war were strange as it did not feel like we were at war. Life went on much as normal. The cafés and restaurants were always full of people, especially on weekends. In the summer the streets and parks were full. The girls always looked so beautiful. They would put down blankets and sunbathe. Before I married I often went to the park on a hot day to sunbathe. I still found time for this when I was married though. The boys would come and sit nearby so that they could stare. They always did that but it never bothered me. The food stores in the city were fully stocked and there was no question of rationing. Life at that time was pretty good for all Germans. There was a sense that Hitler had created this new way of life for us. Of course, we now know that this was not the case.

When my son was born most of my efforts went into keeping the baby and a home. I had my husband to look after, too, so I was quite tired during the first year or so of being a mother. Joachim talked of me having another child straight after the first but I told him "Oh no, you don't. You can keep that torpedo of yours in your own tube for the time being!" I really did not want another child so soon. Joachim always complained at having to use protection when we made love, but I stuck to my guns. As a woman in Nazi Germany they tried hard to remove the luxury of choice from your life. I was not eager at that point to begin a collection of Mother's Crosses.

The 'Mother's Cross' Kitka refers to in her narrative was a decoration, established on 11 December 1938. Officially it was known as 'The Cross of Honour of the German Mother' (*Ehrenkreuz der Deutschen Mutter*). Conferred by the government of the German Reich, it was a civil state decoration. It was awarded in three classes: bronze, silver and gold. A woman bearing five children would receive the bronze, a woman bearing six the silver and a woman who bore seven children would receive the gold award. Although it might appear like an award for the Nazi sexual Olympics, it was designed to encourage German couples to have large families. The Third Reich would need a robust and thriving population if it were to attain the goals that Hitler himself had set. The award of this decoration required exhaustive administrative procedures, therefore it was an award which carried with it a great deal of prestige and respect for its recipients.

As Christmas of 1939 approached life for many Germans continued as before, though the German military was already planning its next operation; to invade France, Belgium, Luxembourg and the Netherlands. The German *Blitzkrieg* (Lightning War) principle of the German army and Luftwaffe working together as a combined force had proved devastatingly effective during the invasion of Poland. The next phase of Germany's plan to conquer Europe would be hinted at within the classrooms of some of the country's schools, as Gertrud Koerg recalled:

German aspirations in Europe from 1939 were discussed and debated in the classroom. I remember vividly the teacher drawing up maps on the board and asking us how we might carry out a surprise attack on an enemy country. He would ask the boys in particular which way they might go about such a task. Some of the theories were quite amusing and not out of place in some second-rate science fiction novel, yet others were surprisingly close to the techniques actually adopted by our armed forces during the invasion of France and the Low Countries. The school master asked which way you would send your army to conquer France. Would you go through roads and fields – an obvious choice, which an enemy may anticipate – or would you choose another method? There was brief silence before one of the girls raised her hand for attention. The schoolmaster ignored her for a minute, looking about the room for a boy to raise a hand, but none of them did. The schoolmaster asked the girl to stand and explain her reasoning. She said to him, "I would push an army through the forests, woods and rivers, sir." The schoolmaster then asked, "And why would you do this?" The girl then went on to explain, "Because no one would expect an army to go through all of that. It is known throughout the ancient world that campaigns have been won through choosing the least obvious military option." The schoolmaster was amazed, even slightly embarrassed, at the girl's theory. He retorted, "Are you sure you have no one in the military who could have already briefed you as to our military planning, girl?" She just shook her head and said, "No, sir, it is merely common sense." The class briefly erupted into laughter before the schoolmaster grabbed his stick and struck one of the desks before him in anger, shouting, "Silence!" He gazed about the room. His face was like stone. Only his eyes moved like that of a lizard eyeing up an insect. He then nodded his head and said, "Hmm, very good. With thinkers like this I should soon be hounded out of my profession, should I not?" We were then excused from class for the afternoon. On the way home I used to walk back from school with my sisters, mother and a friend named Friedrich. Friedrich had an uncle who was a captain or something in the Wehrmacht. He used to say his uncle Herbert was away a lot of the time on some kind of special training with the army. I never really thought to question this at the time, but it all seems so obvious now, doesn't it?

Christmas 1939 was celebrated with much fervour. The Koerg household spared none of the accoutrements associated with the Christmas celebrations in Germany. The house was decorated with various coloured paper streamers, hand-painted hangings and a large Christmas tree that stood in the entrance hall to the house. Helena and Reinhard Koerg loved the wintertime, particularly Christmas, in Germany. As snow began to carpet the landscape they would take their three girls out sledging. Helena wrote of that Christmas in 1939:

This has been a weekend of magic. Today, Christmas day, Monday, 25 1939, has been beautiful. We attended church yesterday morning and the girls were so excited by it all. We have bought them dolls, along with toy prams in which they can be pushed. Gertrud does not want dolls for Christmas this year and has asked for a wristwatch on Santa Claus's list of things she wanted. In the event, she has her wristwatch, along with a small, gold ring purchased from a local jeweller. Gertrud has such slender fingers we were worried the ring may not fit her properly. Reinhard also insisted that the Führer's book should be among our eldest daughter's gifts. So she has a copy of Hitler's *Mein Kampf* also. The girls woke early this morning and they were running excitedly down the stairs at 6am, their white nightgowns flapping behind them in their haste. There were cries of "Mutter! Papa!" Then they asked if they could see if Santa Claus had left them presents. There were shrieks of delight as they saw the three little piles of carefully wrapped gifts beneath the tree in the entrance hall. All that careful gift wrapping was gone in a flurry of excited little hands and flying bits of paper. The young ones were excited with their new dolls and prams. Gertrud was almost moved to tears with her wristwatch. The *Mein Kampf* book by Hitler was examined briefly before being tossed aside to open the small box from myself and Reinhard. Her eyes shone as she untied the ribbon and pulled off the wrapping. She had no idea what was inside the small box so it was a treat to see her face. "Mutter, Papa, oh thank you so much. I adore it," were her words and she slid the little gold ring onto her finger. She looked up and smiled and said, "Here, look, it fits perfectly and I shall never take it off." With the girls happily engrossed in their gifts, myself and Reinhard exchanged ours. I had bought Reinhard a new hat, leather gloves and winter coat with a collar lined with bear's fur. Reinhard had bought me the most beautiful gold necklace with a ruby set within its centre. He had also bought me some gold earrings.

I had been up early this morning and we decided that we were having pork for dinner. This was a joint of meat which was given to us by Reinhard's boss, who was a keen hunter and had shot the boar himself. It was a sizeable joint of meat so I cut it into quarters and put the one piece in to cook slowly. All that was needed now were the vegetables. These were easy to prepare though peeling them was never my favourite task on a Christmas morning.

Mother and father were joining us for dinner and Reinhard's parents were coming too. It was something of a small banquet compared to normal days as sweetmeats had to be baked for the children along with things for supper time. I just prayed there would be no arguing over the war at dinner, today of all days. Our parents were opposing forces on the question of the war. As I prepared the various things for the meal I stood and thought, 'we are at war but what war?' It did not feel like we were at war. Reinhard made the fire and brought logs into the sitting room so we did not have to keep going outside when we needed more. I looked through the gap in the door at the girls. The little ones were on the floor playing with their dolls while Gertrud was sat with her feet up reading the *Mein Kampf* book. She had a puzzled expression upon her face. I was not exactly happy with her reading the book but knew it was unwise for her education to not read it. My mother and father referred to it as a book of political filth. I knew that there would be trouble if it were discovered that Gertrud had received a copy of it. I had to tell her to lie basically and to put it away before the old people arrived for dinner. I was dreading another political confrontation between the in-laws and Reinhard.

Reinhard disappeared down to the local inn, where I suspect he had more than just the two beers he had said he would have. He came back an hour before dinner. I was in the bedroom changing into a dress when he came in as amorous as ever. I told him, "Not now, I have to be ready, you drunken fool!" He protested that he was not drunk at all. I kept trying to put on the dress yet Reinhard pulled it away from me each time I tried to get into it. It got to the point I had to tell him to close the door and slide the bolt across. If I failed to give in to him we would still be messing around up here when our families arrived. I let the dress slip from my hands. I said to Reinhard, "We have only a few minutes so hurry yourself up." He removed the brown leather belt from his trousers, which fell around his ankles. I can see how excited he is. He pulled off his shirt, casting it aside and insisted I kneel down on the bed. The lovemaking was rough, typical of a man operating under the influence of beer. He uttered the words, "I love you. my angel Helena." He leant forward and I felt his mouth and tongue against my back. His biting increased as his excitement mounted. I knew that if a girl tenses her pelvic muscles the man will ejaculate quicker. I tensed my muscles with every ounce of my strength. A few short thrusts and I felt that he had exploded deep within me. I felt the throb and twitch of him ejaculating. He moaned out loudly and the sweat ran off his face like rain off the roof during a thunder storm.

The next thing Gertrud is calling us from the bottom of the staircase that grandpapa and grandmother Koerg have just arrived. I get up from my kneeling position, telling Reinhard, "Go and wash and tidy your hair up before you go downstairs to greet your parents." I certainly do not wish to give them any indication of what we have just done. I put on my underwear quickly followed by the dress and sit before my dressing table preparing my hair. I put on a small amount of perfume before hurrying downstairs. I embrace Reinhard's parents and ask them to join me in the sitting room with the children. The fire is now roaring away and in the kitchen the meat is almost cooked. I pour drinks for Reinhard's parents then I sit down with them while the girls show them their presents. I am sure I am not the only girl that has had to endure that awful feeling of semen running out of me. I can feel it running down the insides of my thighs and I cross my legs. After a few minutes I quickly make my excuse to go to the kitchen and the outside toilet. It is cold out there but I have to wipe myself. When I return Reinhard's parents present the girls with more gifts. They have bought the girls some beautiful dresses and a pair of fine shoes each. I tell them to go and change into their new dresses and shoes. My parents arrive a short while after and yet more gifts are exchanged. My mother and mother-in-law help me to plate up the food while Reinhard pours brandy for the men. We sit down to something of a feast, which will be sorely missed over the following years. We say a prayer before we eat. Afterwards there is much clearing up, which the girls help with.

While the women clean up the men talk. For once there is no arguing over the war. Maybe they think, as we women do, that it might all just come to nothing and that life might go on as normal for us. Only time will tell what will happen. There is no fear or sense of dread or doom at this stage. Germany is very strong and very well defended. For the time being we shall just rejoice and enjoy this wonderful season and coming New Year. What will 1940 hold for us all? At the moment we celebrate as this is the girl's time and I want nothing to upset it for them. The adults are all on their best behaviour, which is something of a miracle in this household. I thank god for that.

Kitka and Joachim Obermann were also celebrating Christmas in the company of her parents at their home. Her aunt, uncle and grandparents were also present. Kitka recalled:

Our reception was not as frosty as the air outside on that Christmas Day in 1939. My mother and father adored our little son, Roel. They were too busy fawning over the boy in competition with the others to express their usual poor attitude towards me. Either way I just wanted dinner to be over with so we could go back home. Joachim felt the same way and we both agreed after dinner and the traditional afternoon walk that we would make our excuses and head back home where we could spend the rest of the day quietly with Roel. Dinner was very good as my mother was, above all else, an excellent cook, if a terrible mother in my eyes. I noticed in the library where we had drinks before dinner there was this huge new oil painting of Adolf Hitler. Joachim remarked, "It must have cost a fortune!" My father stood lovingly before the painting, admiring it and saying, "This is a cultural investment." I made the error of remarking, "That man is nothing more than an ogre." An argument ensued between me and my father. I was sick of him and maybe the wine I had drunk gave me a high degree of courage. Mother came in and broke up the argument, telling us to behave as we were causing a scene in front of our other guests. We ate dinner in relative silence; only the crack of wood burning in the fireplace broke the quiet. My aunt began to make conversation but it was awkward small talk about trivial things. It did alter the mood and before long we were talking mainly about how Roel enjoys the snow and the gifts he has had this year.

After dinner we had the usual walk through the town. It was refreshing after being in the stuffy heat of my parent's home. When we returned from the walk we decided, as planned, to make our excuses and leave for home. I don't think my parents were sorry to see us go. They embraced Roel, kissing him lovingly as most grandparents do. They handed him a small bag of sweet treats, which included some of mother's gingerbread. Mother always gave gingerbread at Christmas time. It was another of her traditions. As we walked home me and Joachim spoke very little about the dinner other than the food was fine. I burst out laughing, which in turn made Joachim laugh. We were in fits of laughter. Joachim said, "I can't help thinking your poor father will report you to the authorities for rubbishing his prize oil painting of our dear Führer." We just laughed all the way home and even Roel began to laugh because we were laughing so much.

Adaline Seidel, an eighteen-year-old from the dirt poor Kreuzberg area of Berlin, had always hated Christmas, despite its huge significance in German culture. Her parents were employed in menial jobs. They rarely had the luxury of surplus income and Adaline's mother Ursula worked herself to the bone, sometimes doing three separate jobs every day of the week apart from Sundays. However, for the Seidel family Hitler's ascent to power probably saved their lives, as Adaline explains:

Before the Nazi government came into being many of us in the Kreuzberg district were suffering from the most appalling poverty. Deaths amongst the young in this poor district were significantly higher than anywhere else. Before the Nazis nobody cared about any of the poor Germans; we were just left to get on with things. In many cases the local men used to say, "We are being left to get on and die". Every winter, particularly Christmas, was extremely depressing and unpleasant for us. The winters were freezing and our home would have ice on the insides of the windows. This would happen because we could not afford to buy coal. My father used to go out and steal wood with his friends.

They once went out at night and ripped someone's wooden picket fencing down to use for fuel on their fires. Our neighbour, God bless her, had four young children and she lost every single one to illness. Two of them died in the winter of 1930, one the following year, and another in 1932. All of them died through a lack of nutrition. Their bodies were just too weak to fight off the infections brought about by the winter conditions.

Both my parents were fervent supporters of the NSDAP, or National Socialist German Workers Party as you know them. They offered a ray of hope to us and their leader, Adolf Hitler, spoke so passionately of the plight of ordinary working-class Germans. Everything steadily changed after 1933. Criminal activity in our district became non-existent. There were no more pitched battles out on the street between those bloody communists and the other rival political gangs. You were scared to leave your doors unlocked for fear of thieving. It was a grim setting for the seeds of hope to be sown. Yet the seeds of hope were sown with Adolf Hitler. As the Nazis set about the task of improving the living conditions of poor and working-class German families, initiatives were introduced to tackle not only the problems of malnutrition but the lack of everyday basic necessities.

I recall one morning in particular when there was all this fuss outside on the street. I looked through the window to see what was going on. I did not go outside with the other neighbours as my mother was ill in bed upstairs. My father was with her, sat by her side to keep an eye on her. As I peered through the milky glass I could make out men in uniforms and a huge black car of some sort. I could hear the shouts of "Heil, heil!" and knew it could mean only one thing, that Hitler was visiting nearby. I was excited but, as I say, I could not go outside. Just a few minutes later there was a knock at our door. When I opened the door I had the biggest shock of my life. There stood Adolf Hitler, the Führer himself, flanked by uniformed soldiers. I was dumbstruck and couldn't speak. My father came running down the stairs to apologise and immediately invited the visitors inside. Father kept apologising for the condition of our home. I think Hitler said to him, "My good man, please, we are not here to carry out an inspection." He had a smile on his face, a warm smile. Hitler asked father where his wife was and father explained she was in bed resting due to illness brought about by severe exhaustion. Hitler and those with him asked how many days father and mother worked and what kind of jobs they were doing. Hitler then asked if he could pass personal greetings to my mother. My father led the party upstairs where they surrounded mother in her bed and each man shook her hand. We were asked what kinds of foods we had been living on and how much we had. We were asked about clothing and coal too. When my father explained we had virtually nothing and mother had no medicine Hitler appeared genuinely concerned and visibly moved. On his way out of our home he and the soldiers with him shook our hands. I was patted on the head and told not to worry and that things would be sorted out.

The week that followed Hitler's visit saw bundles of new clothes, some shoes, coal and foods we could never have afforded arrive at our doorstep. My mother was supplied with the medicines she needed to battle her illness and slowly but surely she improved and gained her fitness to work again. Things were sorted out at the factories where the men like my father worked. The bosses were all made to attend a meeting with representatives of the NSDAP. Apparently they were shouted at and scolded for being mean and allowing their German workers to starve. Many of the factories were brought under the auspices of the Nazi state, and conditions improved and men could earn a proper wage for the skills they possessed. At least every Christmas after Hitler's visit we could eat properly and even have a few treats we would not have previously enjoyed. The factory bosses were generous too and gave us many perks. One of the factory bosses came and gave all the children on our street cakes made of gingerbread. Christmas 1939 was the best ever. One of the industry bosses arranged a special party for the workers' families. It was like a medieval banquet and looked as if no expense had been spared.

At that time, while we were indeed a country at war, we had few worries. What I can say is that if it had not been for Hitler visiting that winter's day my mother would have almost certainly died; that I am sure of. In a sense Hitler saved us and for that I can't find it in my heart to hate him for the things that occurred later. Survival is all about being selfish in some ways. Hitler's greater plans were to fail terribly later on. Why he set out on that particular path I can't tell you. All I can say is under Hitler for a time we could actually live again.

As Christmas 1939 passed by peacefully in Germany without incident many Germans were now looking forward to New Year's Eve. Nazi propaganda minister, Joseph Goebbels, had been preparing a speech to the German nation which was broadcast on radio on 31 December 1939. His speech was congratulatory of the victories secured by Germany's armed forces that year. The war was going well for Germany and Goebbels' speech appeared to paint an optimistic picture for the future. But he also went on to warn his audience that 1940 would be a hard year. The German-Soviet treaty was also strangely absent from the text of his speech. With hindsight, the reasons for this are now painfully obvious, yet this did not appear to concern Soviet dictator, Josef Stalin. Goebbels talked of discarding the chains of slavery imposed by the German defeat of the First World War, announcing that the country was once again ready to be a great power in Europe. He concluded his address to the German nation by saying: 'As we raise our hearts in grateful thanks to the almighty, we ask his gracious protection in the coming year. We do not want to make it difficult for him to give us his blessing. We want to work and fight and say with that Prussian General, "Lord, if you cannot help us or choose not to, we ask at least that you do not help our damned enemies".'

As the hours and minutes ticked away many Germans were busy celebrating the approach of what they believed would be a momentous and historic year for Germany. As clocks all over the country chimed, heralding the start of 1940, there was much cheer. Many believed that

1940 would indeed be the road to greatness. Initially, 1940 would begin positively from a military perspective. Few could have really contemplated that 1940 would also herald the beginning of what would become a rapid slide into the abyss for Nazi Germany. The proposed 'Thousand-year Reich' would last six painful years. The death, murder, and final destruction that were to come would be unrivalled in our human history. Though 1939 had been a year in which many Germans had asked 'War, what war?' 1940 would be a very different year by its end, leaving few with any illusions as to what was coming.

Chapter 3

Hammer Blow

Life for many Germans in the early part of 1940 continued as normal. The children went to school, the parents to work and couples got married. The euphoria of the military successes of the previous year gave the impression that Germany was once again a major power in Europe. Life was good for its citizens, unless of course you belonged to one of the many persecuted groups. As the young were so important to the future of the Third Reich they were rapidly indoctrinated into the Nazi political agenda. Whether the parents agreed with this policy of politically educating their children was of no concern to the authorities. Any teacher found to be less than enthusiastic in the teaching of the National Socialist doctrine was quickly removed from their profession. The mechanics of indoctrinating German society had been in place well before Hitler and the Nazis came to absolute power in Germany. Jews in particular had been subject to violence, murder and all manner of depravations from as early as the late 1920s. Most of what we term anti-Semitism was in existence long before the Nazis and we can trace its origins to the Christian and pre-Christian civilisations of Europe.

Jewish families, such as that of German-born Melitta Jorg, could see the writing was on the wall. Melitta recalled:

> We had left Germany early on, before the Hitler fever, as we called it, really began to affect those of Jewish ancestry. It was quite stupid really as I was born in Germany. I was more German than Hitler was. The fact that there was Jewish ancestry in my father's bloodline sealed our fate in many aspects. Before Hitler's mob could steal my fathers' assets and throw us into a ghetto or camp, and before the violence against Jews really began to become a problem, my father got us out of Germany. By 1940 we were safely in England,

residing between two holiday homes: one in the suburbs of London and one in Scotland. I followed the events that followed with great interest. My father desperately tried to persuade many other family members and friends to join us but they refused to leave. He even offered to pay for everything for them but they still refused to be bullied into leaving it all behind. It was a fatal mistake as many of my family who we left behind we never saw again. My family knew what was coming next. We could see that Germany would attack France and then turn its eagle's claws towards England. Of course, in 1940 many Germans were feeling very good about themselves. They had driven Jews out of their society, virtually razed Poland to a pile of rubble and reunited the German peoples of Europe. The Nazis were redrawing the pre-1918 map of Europe. Only a blind fool could not have guessed Hitler's next move. Had the world acted together more rapidly Hitler and his cronies could have been stopped. There had been plenty of time in which the world could have intervened, but the world did not. Everyone was too busy washing their hands of world peace. As long as that fucking dog does not choose to defecate in my back yard I do not care was the attitude, or so it felt.

As spring gave way to early summer, Kitka Obermann would sometimes walk down to the kindergarten where she would leave her son, Roel, in the capable hands of the young women there. From there she walked the short distance to the park, lay down a blanket and sunbathed for a short while. It was not out of the ordinary for many young women to put on bikinis or swimming attire in the pursuit of catching a tan. Young German women of the time had been educated towards being fit, healthy and beautiful. Kitka Obermann was a beauty with a finely sculpted physique that soon attracted the attention of amorous local young males as she stretched herself out on the blanket to enjoy the warm sunshine. Kitka recalls:

> It was lovely in the park just lying down in the sun and staring up at the endless blue sky. There would be the occasional wisps of cloud and some took on shapes of their

own. They were like nature's art I used to think and I would really drift off into my own thoughts as I lay staring up at the sky. What was going on in the war didn't concern any of us at that point. There were no hardships and all the shops and public houses were operating as normal, and people just carried on with their lives.

As I lay on the blanket with my arms acting as a cushion for my head I heard a group of male voices nearby. I turned my head to the direction of the voices and saw a group of young men sat down together looking my way. They were all giggling like schoolchildren and whispering to each other. After some minutes one of them, a young, blonde-haired fellow, got up and started walking over towards me. At that moment I just thought, 'Oh, god, leave me alone, for heaven's sake.' So he comes over and says, "Good afternoon, fräulein, what a wonderful day it is today." I can't really see his face in the glare of the sun so I sit up. Standing before me is a well-defined and very good-looking young male. I ask him, "Shouldn't you be at work?" to which he replies, "I am at university and I am not working at the moment." My curiosity aroused, I say to him, "Ah, you must be from a wealthy family then." He nods his head and smiles shyly before replying, "Yes, I am afraid so, fräulein." I tell him my name is Kitka, short for Katherine, and stretch my hand out to shake his. His hands are soft and typical of a man who has had a privileged upbringing, having not been soiled or roughened by the hard, menial work that most Germans were subject to. He then introduces himself as Werner and as he does so his friends continue to giggle and whisper between themselves. I am then asked the inevitable question; would I join him for a drink in the nearby café? I raise my left hand so he can see the gold wedding ring on my finger. I apologise to him and tell him, "I can't do that as I have a husband and he would be very angry if he found out I had joined a complete stranger for drinks while half naked." He laughs and asks me if we can, if nothing else, be friends and asks me if I will be here often on sunny days. I tell him I might be and then he offers me his hand again and says,

"Thank you, Kitka. Meeting you today has been an extra ray of sunshine for me." He walks back to his friends and I resume my previous posture and continue my sunbathing. I feel my eyes becoming more and more heavy and drift into a light sleep.

I am only asleep for ten to fifteen minutes. I sit up and look around myself. The group of young men, and Werner, have gone. I have to head back now and get Roel from the kindergarten and return home. I slip a skirt and jacket over my costume and leave the park. I see many girls lounging around in the sun and soldiers in their uniforms walking arm in arm with their wives or girlfriends. It is a happy scene to end the day and the walk to the kindergarten and home is invigorating. I wish the days could be like this forever, and maybe they will. The young man, Werner, who had come and introduced himself earlier that day does not figure immediately in my thoughts. Yet, as evening comes I find myself thinking about him. I know it is wrong but I can't help myself reminiscing and thinking things I should not be thinking.

Helena Koerg's brother, Peter, paid an unexpected visit one Saturday in early May of 1940. While he was composed in many respects his mood appeared excited, if somewhat agitated. Helena recalls:

He was like a cat on hot coals. He was pacing and couldn't sit down and was obviously excited about something. He just told me that something big was going to happen soon and that he would be playing a forward role, but he could say no more and I was not to tell anyone outside the home about what he had said. He then explained he would be away for a while, maybe some months, and wanted to see the girls and Reinhard before he left. I had my suspicions of what he was trying to tell me. As I called the girls in from the garden I said to him, "Look, you be careful. Whatever you are going into it is not a game." He promised he would be careful and would be in touch with us all at the first opportunity. I knew it was something to do with the war and I had an idea the army and Luftwaffe were planning an operation to attack somebody, but who? I really had no idea at the time and as I hugged Peter before he left to go and visit mother and father, I again told him, "Don't do anything stupid, Peter. Dead heroes are worth nothing you know." He asks where I got such an absurd statement from and I just smile in reply and let him go on his way. Of course, that phrase I used was one taken from the lips of old Herr Fauschner, the baker. If anyone understood the futility of war, Herr Fauschner did.

Gertrud Koerg also recalls that visit from a very excited Uncle Peter:

We were out playing in the garden when mother called us in as Uncle Peter had arrived to see us. We did not see him that much since he had been involved in training with the German air force. I did not even know what kinds of planes he had learned to fly. He always used to say, "I will tell you about them next time." Maybe he was not allowed to tell anyone at the time, I don't know. Anyway, we ran to the back door of the house and he hugged and kissed us one by one. When it was my turn, he said, "My beautiful Gertrud," as he hugged me. He said he was going away for a while but when he returned he would bring us some presents. I wanted to know what kinds of presents he would get us and where would they be from. He just said, "I can't tell you right now. Besides, it wouldn't be a surprise if I told you now, would it?" I remember him embracing mother before he left. When father came home mother told him about Uncle Peter's visit and what he had said. We were not permitted to sit in and listen to our parents' conversation but it was clear something was happening; something pretty big.

The rhetoric and propaganda being broadcast across Germany as May 1940 approached should have been warning enough of her intentions, particularly in Western Europe. Germany had been flexing her muscles for some time, forcing the British into planning for a possible war with Germany. The British Expeditionary Force (BEF) sailed to France in September 1939 and began to assemble along the Belgian-French border.

For the most part the British soldiers were preoccupied with the task of digging trenches and field defences. At the time the British referred to this period as the 'Phoney War' and many doubted that a German attack would ever come.

When the German attack did come, on 10 May, it came as a hammer blow; one that left British and French forces reeling. Employing their *Blitzkrieg* tactics of troops, armour and air force all working together as a combined force, the Germans began to pulverise the British and French forces, who were then forced to retreat through Belgium and northwestern France in the face of such a sustained bombardment. The BEF, French and Belgian forces found themselves cut off north of the River Somme. Pursued by German troops, armour, artillery and the Luftwaffe, the bedraggled forces headed for the French coastal town of Dunkirk. With the English Channel as their only escape route, the Allies were trapped and at the mercy of German air forces. A rescue effort was immediately put in motion in the form of the Operation Dynamo. Ships and boats of all sizes, both civilian and military, were procured along with their crews in a combined effort to save as many soldiers as possible from the besieged beaches of Dunkirk. As the fleet of rescue ships and boats approached the beaches they came under sustained attack from the Luftwaffe. The Junkers Ju87 'Stuka' dive bombers fell from the skies above Dunkirk like gannets, targeting the rescue ships as they made their way to and from Dunkirk.

Hitler could quite easily have ordered his *Panzer* (tank) forces to annihilate the trapped enemy forces in Dunkirk, yet, for reasons unknown, he hesitated. This was the first major military error of the Second World War that Hitler would make. Had he ordered his forces onto the beaches of Dunkirk the British, French and Belgian troops trapped there would have been killed or captured. Had that occurred the D-Day invasion of 6 June 1944 could not have taken place. Hitler's folly had allowed a significant proportion of the BEF to escape home across the English Channel. In their wake they left behind thousands of guns, along with ammunition and other supplies, most of which would later be utilised by the Germans. While France fell the British were reluctant to commit further military forces to what was now a futile effort. Even the Royal Air Force was withdrawn from the skies over France. The British were painfully aware that they would need every available Spitfire and Hurricane fighter for the possible battle to come. As France fell the German forces reaped the spoils of war.

Helena Koerg's brother, Peter Marschmann, was now a fighter pilot assigned to *Jagdgeschwader* 51 (*Jagd* means 'hunt' and *Geschwader* means 'wing'). With the rank of *Gefreiter* (Private First Class) he flew the Messerschmitt Bf109E, which was regarded as a formidable adversary. After France was defeated, the German fighter and bomber pilots were able to take a rest from offensive operations. Many of the pilots, along with soldiers of the *Wehrmacht*, enjoyed their time in France. They frequented the many cafés, bars and restaurants and engaged in sightseeing as if holidaymakers on a summer break. The French were forced to sign the German surrender terms in the same railway carriage that the Germans had been forced to sign the surrender terms in 1918. Hitler had insisted that the carriage be moved from the museum where it had been on display since the end of the First World War. He then showed his contempt for the French by leaving before proceedings had been completed. Hitler was ecstatic over the defeat of the French, but he had further territorial gains in mind.

Peter Marschmann sat down and wrote a letter to his sister, Helena, back in Germany. Helena received his letter a couple of weeks later. He wrote:

> Dear Sister, by the time you receive this letter you will have heard of what a fantastic victory we have achieved. Our Luftwaffe is the best air force in the world. The French were no match for our Messerschmitts. I have a great surprise to reveal that I shot down my first enemy aircraft during our invasion. I don't think he even saw me coming. I attacked from above and behind, out of the sun. The Frenchman was flying a Bloch series fighter. In a few seconds of cannon fire he was tumbling out of the sky. I followed him down and watched as he cartwheeled along a field. By the time he stopped there was little more than flaming lumps of debris spread across the field. The Frenchman had not attempted to leave his machine during combat. Now we enjoy a rest and see some of the sights, including the Eiffel Tower, where we are going tomorrow. I will find some gifts for my beautiful nieces and please pass my love to them all and regards to Reinhard. I will be back to visit as soon as I am permitted time. Take care of yourselves and please don't worry about us here as all will be well.

Peters signs off with 'Love always from your brother Peter'. Helena excitedly showed Peter's letter to the girls, who fought for the chance to read it out. Gertrud, being the oldest, received the privilege of reading its contents to her younger siblings. She begs her mother to let her take her uncle's letter to school the next day so that her class can also hear the news. Helena reluctantly agrees to let Gertrud take the letter, providing she never lets it out of her sight. Gertrud describes the reaction of her class in school the following day:

> Oh, they were so envious. None of the other girls had an uncle or relative who was a fighter pilot. As I read out the letter the teacher listened, deep in thought, his head balanced upon his knuckles. He smiled as I read the brief description of my uncle's battle with the French aircraft. When I finished reading there was a huge cheer from the whole class, who were told to stand and say, "Heil Hitler". The teacher then drew a map on the board, explaining the latest territorial gains. He then said, "We are now at a buffer zone of the French coast. England is all but a short journey across the water. With God's blessing, in a few months' time the territories we now own will include that of England too." After the letter reading we had to recite some passages from *Mein Kampf*. Our teacher told us the teachings in the pages of this wonderful text were an omen of Germany's greatness. We should all be proud, work hard and carry out every task required of us in the coming struggle. He reaffirmed that there would be struggle. There can never be war without struggle, he explained, but we will prevail. It was Wednesday and on Wednesday evenings I had to attend the *Jungmadelbund*. I took the letter with me to the evening meeting, where its content caused much excitement. After that I had even more girls wanting to be my friend. Yes, it felt brilliant, I have to admit.

With Germany now in control of France and the Low Countries Hitler turned his attention towards the island across the English Channel. Invasion barges had been transported to the coast in preparation for what was known as 'Operation Sea Lion': the invasion of England. A seaborne invasion was considered a last resort if all other options failed. Hitler had hoped that, in the wake of the fall of France, the British would seek a peace agreement with Germany. He understood that the British Royal Navy was a formidable force compared to the limited size of the German *Kriegsmarine* (navy) and there was no question of the German navy contesting the waters of the English Channel and North Sea. Therefore the responsibility of bringing about suitable conditions for a seaborne invasion of England fell to the Luftwaffe. They would, in effect, be going it alone in the next phase of Hitler's planning. It was decided that the German air force would attack shipping convoys and ports.

As the war effort against England was increased the air campaign began to target RAF airfields and other British military infrastructure such as aircraft production facilities. From 10 July to 31 October 1940 the Luftwaffe found itself locked in a desperate struggle to achieve superiority in the skies over England. It was the first time the German air force had entered into battle as an independent force. There could be no army, tanks or artillery to accompany it across the Channel. Initially, the Luftwaffe tactics were proving successful. The men and machines of Britain's Royal Air Force soon found themselves under considerable pressure. It was a frightening time to be a citizen in the UK, especially in the south of England, where many residents witnessed the daily air battles high above them. Each day the Luftwaffe attacked in huge formations of fighters and bombers and each time the RAF were there to greet them in steadfast defence of the freedom of its people. RAF Fighter Command, however, did not have endless reserves of Hurricanes and Spitfires. something would have to give. One or the other side would have to break at some point in what had become a battle of attrition. The momentum shifted decisively in Britian's favour when the disorientated crew of a German bomber jettisoned its bombs over southern England. The date was 22 August 1940 and the bombs fell on the Harrow and Wealdstone areas, which were technically outside London within the city's Civil Defence area. At this stage of the battle Hitler forbade the bombing of British cities. However, this one act would bring about the end of any concept of a gentlemanly air war.

Alicia Beremont, a twelve-year-old French girl, recalled the swarms of German fighters and bombers taking off from their airfields situated around the French countryside:

> They reminded me of flying ants taking to the air on a warm summer's night. I used to watch them from the boundary of my parents' dairy farm. Once they had taken off they would circle around then head off towards the direction of England. I used to time them to see how long it took them to come back. The fighters always returned first as they did not have the fuel to remain with the bombers for very long. When the bombers did return some would be on fire and trailing tunnels of thick, black smoke behind them. I once watched as one of them disappeared behind some trees near our farm. I think the pilot was trying to come down in one of our fields. He struck the treetops, which sort of spun his aircraft around, and it crashed and exploded into flames. There was the cracking sound of bullets exploding in the fire. No one got out of that aeroplane alive. They were all burned to death. I did not feel sorry for the Germans back then and I felt like cheering, but knew I couldn't in case I was seen. The Germans I encountered were always polite and did us no harm but this was our country not theirs.

Helena and Reinhard Koerg received another letter from Helena's brother, Peter. In it he invited them to come and stay in Paris for a weekend as he had some weekend leave planned. Helena recalled:

> We hastily packed some clothes and things for the girls and caught the first train. We stopped off overnight as it was a long journey for the girls. Peter had planned to meet us and pick us up in a car and take us to a hotel in Paris. It was the first time I had seen Peter in what seemed a long while. He looked a little pale and underweight and seemed to have lost his usual enthusiasm. He talked little of the war he was engaged in and from his silence I gathered things were not going quite to plan. He just kept saying, "We are getting on with it." The girls were pleased to see him and asked if he

had presents for them. In the event he took them around the shops and bought them some items of clothing and ice cream. The girls seemed to lift his mood so it was not a bad break in all. I had been to Paris before with my parents but the girls had never been before so it was an adventure for them. Sadly, the weekend was over all too quickly. Peter gave us a lift in his car as far as he could and from there we caught the train back to Kassel. As we embraced and said our farewells I asked Peter, "If there is anything wrong you promise not to keep it from me. If anything is troubling you please tell me now." He stood there, silent for a minute, then embraced me again and just said quietly in my ear, "Helena, my dear sister, I don't think we are going to win this war." He was almost in tears, especially when the girls had to say goodbye to him. We left him standing by the car and walked to get the train back home. For the journey back home I was silent in my own thoughts. The girls and Reinhard slept, the bobbing motion of the carriage having the effect of a lullaby upon their tired bodies. I couldn't think what Peter could have meant by what he said to me as we parted. The propaganda back home says we are winning the war against England. I am worried for the first time since all this started and I fear for my dear brother's safety.

Although it had been suggested that a Luftwaffe raid took place on London on the afternoon of 16 August 1940, it was the later, inadvertent bombing of London by a Heinkel He111 crew that prompted British prime minister, Winston Churchill to issue a retaliatory air attack on Berlin. During the night of 25 August 1940, RAF aircraft were dispatched to bomb the German capital. The targets were the aerodrome at Tempelhof, near the centre, and Siemensstadt. Ursula Bomme, who was eighteen at the time, lived between Dahlem and Steglitz. She recalled the RAF raid that occurred on the night of 25 August 1940:

The RAF planes had obviously been detected as the air raid warning began to sound. We did what most German families did and went down into the cellar beneath our house. As we made our way down the steps my father commented,

"This must be some sort of drill or exercise. No enemy plane can surely reach us here in Germany." As we settled down and waited, thinking this was all some kind of mistake, the sound of distant anti-aircraft fire could be heard. The sound grew steadily in volume and ferocity. As the planes came closer the anti-aircraft guns nearest us began to fire on the planes. Soon all of the guns in and around the city were firing away. It was the most intense, loudest noise I had ever heard in my life to that point. The noise of the guns was so intense that I do not recall hearing bombs fall or the engines of any aircraft.

The Berlin anti-aircraft defences had been so heavy that the guns had forced the attacking RAF bombers to higher altitudes, which made their bombing considerably less accurate. As a result, that first raid on Hitler's capital proved relatively inconclusive. None of the RAF's intended targets were hit or even damaged. Most of the bombs fell in fields and woods, though some residential areas were hit. The damage was only slight and no one had been killed. In the eyes of many, such an operation would have been considered a failure. Yet, from a psychological point of view, it was a huge success. So much so that it forced Hitler into changing his strategy during the Battle of Britain. This was the second of a series of tactical interferences with military matters that would cost Germany the Second World War. Incensed at the British attack on his beloved Berlin, Hitler flew into a terrible rage. He vowed vengeance on the British, promising that Germany would raze British cities to the ground. But Hitler had been naïve to think that Germany would remain impervious to attack from the air. Luftwaffe chief Hermann Göring had also made a ridiculous boast that no enemy aircraft would ever fly over the Reich territory.

Gertrud Koerg recalls the reaction of her grandfather to this first bombing raid on Germany by the RAF:

We used to have what I called my 'Conversations with Grandpapa'. When I used to see my grandparents on a weekend my grandpapa and I would always talk when away from the other family members. I recall my grandpapa saying to me, "The English will not go down without putting up a good fight. They have proved that they can reach us with their bomber aircraft. Göring said that would never happen and if it did we could call him Meyer. Well, maybe he will be delighted to be called Meyer but what good is that going to do us. The English planes will be back we can be sure of that. Soon people will be dying in their thousands." The old man sat in the chair, looking into my eyes very deeply with tears filling his eyes. I knew that the things grandpapa was saying could be considered treason by the state. His greying blue eyes had seen and witnessed so much over the years of his life. He was no fool and for the first time I began to sense a slight feeling of fear about what was going to happen in this war. He told me, "You, my child, are one of my most precious things in this world, don't let them make you how they are. Please don't let them take your soul away from you with their poison." It was something that gave me much to think about. I was old enough to understand right and wrong. That one should not abuse another human for being different to us, or maybe having different ideas to us. The problem was it had been happening for so long in Germany that it was considered normal to hate everything non Germanic. I was, of course, proud being a pure German, yet if the time came could I be violent, aggressive, pitiless and ruthless? I really didn't know and I just felt torn between my instincts as a human being and of being a loyal and obedient servant to our nation. We had, as a nation, delivered a hammer blow to Poland, the French and the British. As yet the blood of our nation had not made our grip upon that hammer slippery.

Chapter 4

A View of Heaven Through a Bullet Hole

As the long, hot summer of 1940 came to an end a young French girl named Giselle Durand, who lived in the town of Calais, noted the change in the German activities in the port.

Our little town was once subject of much German military activity. The Germans had brought in these barges ready to invade England. There were once many hundreds of German soldiers in the town and billeted in the surrounding areas. The air battles of 1940 were quite visible from where we were. We saw the Germans crossing the English Channel. Sometimes there would be hundreds of aircraft in the sky all heading towards England. It was common to see German planes flying back low over the water with smoke trailing from their engines. They flew so low you could even see all the bullet holes in their aircraft. These damaged aircraft would land at local fighter bases in the Calais region. I remember seeing a German plane flying low over the water with an engine on fire. The Germans shouted at me and told me to go inside my home. They did not want us French seeing them defeated. I was elated to see their planes limping home with flames coming out of them.

I was not exactly a child at that time. I was seventeen years old. I worked for my family in one of the many cafés in our town. The German's used to come in all the time and drink our coffee and wine. My father once laughed after serving a group of German Luftwaffe officers. I asked him what was so amusing. He later told me quite bluntly that he had "pissed in the wine that the German's had drunk". We had heard small pieces of information through the

French resistance that the Germans had lost many aircraft trying to defeat the English. When the invasion barges slowly began to disappear we guessed that things had not gone as the Germans had planned. Their planes would still head for England in large formations but they had changed their tactics. We heard they had abandoned their plans to invade England in favour of bombing England's cities. It was said they would bomb England into submission with a sustained air campaign against English cities. I just thought to myself, "English people please be brave; stand up to these beasts as they can and will be beaten.

Indeed the Germans had changed tactics, spurred on by Hitler's desire for revenge. The Luftwaffe began to attack London in a bombing campaign that became known as 'The Blitz'. It was fortunate for the British that time that Hitler had not discovered just how close the Luftwaffe were to defeating the RAF. Had they continued their campaign against the RAF and its airfields for another two to three weeks, they would have secured air superiority over England.

When Helena Koerg's brother, Peter, returned home on a brief period of leave in late August of 1940 Helena was shocked at his appearance:

My brother called to visit and he looked terrible. He had lost weight and looked pale and gaunt. I said to him, "What the hell have they been putting you through?" He explained that he was being removed from fighter duties and was going to be transferred to a bomber unit. When I asked him why he could not give me a coherent answer and I admit I became annoyed with him. Reinhard heard the change of tone in my voice and came in to see what was going on. Peter covered his face with his hands and began to sob. I felt a sudden rush of guilt at losing my temper with my dear brother. I sat beside him and consoled him and begged him to tell me what the matter was. The girls came running in, excited as usual, and I had to send them outside, telling them uncle Peter needed to talk to mother and father. The girls were disappointed but went out into the garden to play. Peter then began to explain how the Luftwaffe had attacked the British time and again.

"We watched as our bomber aircraft went in, waiting for the Spitfire and Hurricane aircraft of the RAF to attack them. We would wait above the bomber formations and attack the defending fighters as they climbed to attack the bombers. The problem was we had just minutes to try and defend our bomber crews before we had to head back to our airfields. The Me109 does not hold enough fuel for the flight across the channel and then engage the English fighters for any useful length of time. We had to turn back and leave our comrades to the mercy of those Spitfires and Hurricanes. I feel so frustrated at this and the fact that we have lost some very good pilots. Every mission our pilots shoot down British planes yet more appear the next day. I crash-landed an aircraft on three consecutive occasions. They told me my nerves were being shot up worse than my aircraft. They made me take a medical examination. The doctor concluded I have problems with my nerves and he suggested I leave fighter operations and transfer to the bombers. It was more an order than a suggestion. I am to join the bombers as a gunner or something. The only other alternative is to join a flak regiment or something."

Helena did her best to console her brother who was clearly very upset, and after sending him upstairs to wash the tears from his face she called the girls in to see him. Gertrud was first in through the door, hugging her uncle Peter quickly, followed by her two younger sisters. The young man, momentarily mobbed by his young nieces, appeared to forget his wartime troubles. Gertrud recalls the visit:

I didn't say anything but I could see he had been crying. His eyes were red and he had red streaks down his face. I wasn't sure what the problem had been but sensed how happy he was to see us. Naturally, we asked questions about the war but mother and father quickly told us not to ask such questions as uncle Peter wants to forget the war while he is home. She told us this in a nice manner and of course we obeyed her. Peter had some food with us and then left to visit a girl he had been writing to. He didn't tell us who she was at that time but before he left he hugged me and said jokingly, "No girl will ever come before my adorable Gertrud."

Kitka Obermann had a relatively carefree summer of 1940. She had little interest in the war and did not even bother to read the newspapers that her husband Joachim threw down on the dinner table each day. Joachim talked incessantly about the war, especially as the company he worked for was a major producer of armaments. Joachim began to spend more and more time at work and less with his young wife and child. Kitka began writing a journal to pass the time. She also began working odd hours at the kindergarten her son attended. On fine sunny days she would head to the park to sunbathe. She always went to the same spot and had caught the attention of a young man from the town who constantly looked out for her on those warm, sunny days. In her journal she wrote:

Joachim spends so much time at the factory these days that he is hardly ever at home with me and Roel. It makes me angry as I want to spend time with him, away from all the talk about facts, figures and statistics of war production. It's all so damned boring. Today was so fine and sunny. I took Roel to the kindergarten and went to the park. It feels so wonderful to just lie in the warm sun in the open air without a care in the world. I had barely been sunbathing for an hour when I heard the voice of the local boy, Werner. I was actually quite pleased to hear him but I pretended to be asleep. I deliberately tensed my stomach to appear as sexy as I possibly could as I lay on my blanket. As I sensed him coming nearer, he called out, "Good morning, Katherine. How good it is to see you." I removed my sunglasses and replied, "My name is Kitka, not Katherine." He sat down a respectable distance away and asked me how I had been and things like that. It was refreshing that he never spoke about the war. In fact, the subject was only mentioned when I told him where my husband Joachim worked. Then I grumbled about how neglected I am due to the war effort. Werner laughed to the point where I told him off and said, "It is not funny." He then said, "Well, if you were mine I would not leave you at home like that." I smiled at him but reminded him things are not as easy as that. He replied philosophically that life is as complicated as we as individuals make it. I couldn't help but feel attracted to this young man. I got a slight feeling in my stomach every time Werner talked and smiled. He had a reassuring and surprisingly mature attitude and personality. I could see by the way he looked at me that he liked me. As I got up and pack away my blanket I couldn't help but tease him. As I knelt down to roll up the blanket my movements were quite deliberate and designed to fill his mind with thoughts of an erotic nature. I'm sure as he departed there was a bulge in his trousers. I thought to myself, if only I was a single girl I might be very tempted indeed. He shouted to me, "Take care, Kitka, and I hope you will be here again soon."

I collected Roel from the kindergarten and we headed home. Me and Roel had dinner alone as Joachim was working late at the factory again. When he arrived home all he did was eat his dinner and moan about the other people he works with. Then he fell asleep in his chair for an hour or so. By the time he woke up Roel is in bed and I have cleared the dinner things and put them away. When we retire to bed there is no love making as he falls fast asleep and snores so loudly it keeps me awake. I lie awake and think of that boy Werner. As hard as I try my thoughts become erotic. I imagine him making love to me on the blanket in the park. This is not good at all and I know it is wrong of me to be thinking these things. I am just a normal woman. Why should I be different just because I am a German woman and Hitler says, "This is how you will behave and what you will do," and things like that. It's all so fucking unfair.

By September of 1940 the sustained aerial bombardment of London – the Blitz – had begun and would not abate until mid-May 1941, when much of Germany's air force was sent east in preparation for Operation Barbarossa, the invasion of Soviet Russia, though this did not mean that the Luftwaffe bombing campaign against England would cease completely. It was in March of 1941 that the Koerg family received some particularly devastating news. Gertrud Koerg vividly remembers that day as if it were yesterday:

> We were all at home apart from father and it was a Saturday afternoon when my grandpapa called in. He rarely visited on a Saturday as he would always come on Sundays with grandma. He arrived in a terrible state and immediately mother sent us upstairs to play. We were upstairs when I heard my mother scream; a terrible scream that pierced the air in the house and filled me and my sisters with a chill of fear. I wanted to run downstairs to see what was wrong. Instead I shouted from the top of the stairs, "Mother, grandpapa! What is the matter? What is wrong?" I began to cry as I was frightened and next thing grandpapa came up and he took me into mother and father's bedroom. I knew something terrible was wrong and thought maybe grandma was ill or something. Grandpapa sat me down, held my hands and just told me, "It's uncle Peter. He has gone missing." I asked him, "What do you mean, grandpapa, he's gone missing? Where has he gone missing?" Grandpapa then broke down and cried as he tried to explain that uncle Peter's plane had been involved in an operation over England. His plane had made the flight and dropped bombs around the London dockyard areas. They were on the return flight across the North Sea when they were pursued by an enemy plane. The crew of another plane, one of ours, saw my uncle Peter's plane crash down into the sea. The observer could not tell if anyone got out of the aircraft. A rescue plane had been sent out and a German submarine had been in the area and was looking, but there was no further news. Grandpapa explained that uncle Peter may be alright and may have been able to escape by inflating the dinghy boat they had stowed in the bomber he was flying in. He told me not to give up hope, for my mother's sake.
>
> When my father arrived home the news was broken to him. I remember him sitting with his head in his hands after being told. Me and my sisters were taken over to grandpapa and grandma's house, where we stayed for a

few days. Mother was not well at all and she must have suffered something of a nervous breakdown as we stayed at our grandparents for nearly three weeks after. My father came to visit us every day and told us we could return once mother was well enough. I took a few days away from school and when I returned to school the class had made a wreath of remembrance and the teacher had the class salute the wreath. It felt very surreal and in my heart I knew that uncle Peter was never going to return to us and that he was dead. It was confirmed soon after that there had been no survivors in his Dornier bomber. The aircraft sank rapidly with its four crew still inside. My mother had received a letter confirming the plane went into the sea and although the area was thoroughly searched, no survivors were located and all were presumed dead or missing in action.

This brought home the reality of war to me in a very personal sense. I felt very angry at the British and it just made me more determined to help fight the war against them in any way I could. My mother changed too. She did not seem the same after that. She would spend long periods of time staring at uncle Peter's picture on the table in the living room. At the next Jungmadelbund meeting I attended on the Wednesday evening the group saluted me as a tribute to a fallen German in the service of the Reich. I was called to give a brief talk about my uncle. Before I went up in front of the other girls our group leader told me, "Do not cry. Do not show that you are hurting within. Be strong and be proud as Germany will suffer many more sacrifices like yours before this war is won."

Helena Koerg never forgot the last few memories of her dear brother. His death haunted her. Fighting back the tears, she recalled the last time she saw him before he joined the Luftwaffe bomber group *Kampfgeschwader* 2 (KG2):

He said he would be safer flying with the bomber boys, as he called them. He said he would be alright and that maybe we could all meet up again in Paris when he had his next leave after operations. His death hit me very hard as we did not even have a grave to visit and lay down some flowers. My dear brother's grave is somewhere at the bottom of the sea. I know Gertrud often cried at night because I heard her. Peter adored all of our girls but Gertrud was always his favourite as she was his first niece. He loved her so much and she adored him like a hero in return. I would go to the girls' room and quietly ask her if she was alright when I heard her crying. She would always say, "Mother, I am fine, I just had a bad dream that is all." Our two younger girls still found it hard to grasp the concept that lives are lost in war. Both of them began wetting their beds, so I knew they were troubled. Their school was telling them to be tough and not to show emotion, to hate our enemies and to assist by growing into pure German mothers. One of the officers from KG2 visited us not long afterwards. He said that Peter did his job well and was very much liked by those who knew him and the friends he flew with. He brought a few possessions which had been cleared from Peter's personal box at the airfield. All that was left was some clothing and a wristwatch our mother and father bought for him the last Christmas. It was not much with which to remember a dear brother.

I was unwell for some weeks afterwards. I could not stop crying and lost interest in food and everything around me. I had to receive specialist help and was sent to a sanatorium a few miles away for rest while the girls were sent to my mother and father's. Reinhard stayed in the home and went to work. He was dreadfully upset but that man was a real rock to his family and I am so proud of how he coped under all the pressure he must have been under. It did show us we could never be immune from the war; that it could come anytime and take us as quickly as that. After recovering from my brother's loss I wanted to become more involved in work towards the war. They wouldn't let me though. They said, "Look, my dear Fräulein Koerg, if you want to help have another two or three babies; that is the best service you as a young woman can do for your fatherland."

Danni Foestahl was a twenty-two-year-old girl who worked as a hairdresser in the city of Emden. Many of her clients came from the wealthy sector of Emden society. Danni earned a respectable living in the city and enjoyed the freedom of being single while earning good money. She recalls:

> I was really enjoying my life at that time. I had bought my own place with my parents' help and I had a pet daschund which shared my apartment in the suburbs of the city. Every morning, from Monday to Saturday, I would cycle to the hairdresser where I worked. It was only a small salon but was a high fashion place at the time and frequented by the wealthy women of the city. These women were the wives of rich German industrialists and councillors, things like that. They were very wealthy and always paid more than they should for good service, I think you call it tips in your country. Single girls of my age back then were constantly asked if they were going to marry. If we said 'no' then we would be asked why. People with links to the authority would ask you all kinds of questions, even about your sexuality. Of course I had boyfriends, and I liked having them; I just was not very keen on marrying and having children right at that time, when the state said I should settle down and marry and have kids. Things were quite carefree for us, until the first time our beautiful city was bombed by Britain's Royal Air Force. That came as a shock I can tell you. It was in late March [Monday, 31 March was the actual date] when the RAF attacked. On that night the bombers came and dropped these very large bombs on our city.

The bombs Danni refers to were the first operational deployment of the four-thousand-pound high capacity explosive bomb. These large bombs consisted of welded steel cylinders approximately 7.9mm thick. The casings were deliberately thin in order to increase the explosive filling. The bombs were filled with seventy five per cent Amatol as opposed to fifty per cent. Known in RAF slang as a 'cookie', they destroyed purely by their tremendous blast and the resulting incendiary effects rather than the lower-yield blast and fragmentation of the smaller explosive bombs normally used by the RAF. Danni continues:

> These big bombs did considerable damage to factories, storage areas and civilian dwellings. I recall the next morning on my way to work I could see what were once buildings still smouldering. They were just piles of broken bricks and wood. The buildings which did remain relatively intact had their roofs blown clean off. Windows had been shattered over a wide area. There were some streets that were sealed off which we could not go up. Thankfully, the salon I worked at had not been damaged, apart from one shattered window. This was boarded up and we carried on business as usual. I later did some reading on these weapons after the war. It seemed we in Emden were merely guinea pigs to gauge the potential of such big bombs. I can tell you from personal experience that these large bombs were very effective. I know that after the first attack people would come into the salon and talk about what they had seen or heard. The victims of those bombs were never found as most had been blown to tiny pieces. For us in Emden much worse was yet to come although we didn't really realize it at the time. The terrors that were to come were indescribable. As the war intensified for us we began to volunteer for fire service and any work in which we could help the community. After a certain point it was almost impossible to work on a normal basis. The salon [...] was later destroyed by bombing and the infrastructure of the city slowly began to collapse. After that it was a case of just trying to survive. Many of us took to spending hours on end hiding below ground in damp, dark cellars. Others moved away from the city altogether into the countryside to become what were effectively rural refugees.

We will hear more of Danni Foestahl's recollections of her life later. Kitka Obermann's life, meanwhile, was also about to change as the summer of 1941 approached. During the long winter she had often stayed at home, or divided her time between visiting her parents and in-laws and taking her son Roel to the local school. As the warm sun returned she resumed her visits to the park. Over the winter months she had all but forgotten about the young man named Werner who she had met the previous summer. She wrote in her diary:

> I headed for my first visit of the year to the park feeling a slight air of anticipation. I was quite excited at the prospect that the young man I had met months ago might still frequent the park on warm days. As I kicked off my sandals and placed the blanket on the ground I felt somewhat liberated from the months of being housebound, cooking, washing and cleaning and then having to listen to my husband talking about his day at the Dornier works and the wonderful new machines he was helping to build. I lay down on the blanket [...] and I stared up at the blue sky above, as I had done so many times in the past. Occasionally I would look about the park and notice the admiring glances of young men as they passed by. I closed my eyes but was soon roused by a familiar voice calling out to me, accompanied by the sound of a ringing bell. Perched upon a brand-new red bicycle was Werner.
>
> He looked comical sat upon this new bicycle and he kept ringing this little bell attached to the handlebars. I just laughed at him as he looked so amusing. He had a bottle of something tucked under his arm and I asked him what he was doing and where he was going. He replied, "I was hoping that you might allow me to share this bottle of good German wine with you. Of course, if you'd rather not I will understand." I asked him to come over and he almost dropped and tripped over his new bike in his haste. As always, he sat a few feet away from me [...]. I patted the ground beside me and told him, "Come and sit here, you silly fool." He then asked, "Is that a wise idea? What about if your husband hears of this? He might be very angry with me and you. I don't want you to get into any trouble." I reassured him that it was okay and to come and sit with me, which of course he did with no further hesitation. He sat down beside me and nervously pulled the cork out of the wine bottle. He managed to spill some of it on his white

shirt, which made me laugh at him again. He apologised for not having any cups and said, "We will have to drink this straight from the bottle. I know it's not very ladylike for you but if you insist I will go and get some cups from somewhere." I said to him, "For God's sake, just give me that bloody bottle." I then looked around to make sure no one was watching before taking a gulp of the wine. The wine tasted good and by the time we had finished the bottle, which was not long, I felt a little bit pissed. We then talked as it was easier to talk about personal things when you have had a drink.

I told him about how bored and unappreciated I felt. I loved my husband but I felt we had drifted apart as it felt like he had chosen his career over me and Roel. I explained how I felt it was all so unfair. Werner told me that he had been dating a local girl but her father took a dislike to him, forcing her to end their relationship. For a few seconds his face changed and I thought he would start crying. I don't know why I did it but I placed my hand beneath his chin and lifted his head up. I then kissed him on the lips. He seemed shocked for a few seconds then he just wrapped his arms around me and kissed me passionately on the mouth. As we kissed I felt his tongue probing my mouth. I had not felt this excited in a very long time. I felt desired and wanted and it was nice. Soon we were both lying down and Werner almost climbed on top of me. I said to him, "No, not here. Can we go somewhere else?"

At that point I no longer cared. Werner quickly picked up his bike while I rolled up the blanket and threw my coat around myself. Werner then took me across the park, where we both crawled through a hedge into a deserted spot surrounded by thick bushes and trees. I threw down the blanket and we began kissing again. He soon removed my bathing top and bottoms, kissing my mouth, neck and breasts as we both lay down. I felt him move in between my legs as I opened my thighs for him. I was seeing stars as he began to enter me and make love to me. It felt so nice. I had almost forgotten what it felt like to have a man who felt so much desire inside me. He was a considerate lover and as his pace quickened within me I felt that steadily building, tingling feeling deep within my womanhood. I couldn't help it and cried out so loud he had to put his hand over my lips. Seconds later he climaxed and I felt him ejaculating deep within me. It was a strange, erotic, yet warm feeling. We both lay there, looking at each other for a few minutes. I felt him begin to harden within me again and told him I would have to go now. As he began yet more steady strokes I could not resist and fell back into that wonderful feeling. He climaxed inside me again and as soon as he had finished I managed to roll him off me, fearing we would be there all day if I did not. I quickly rolled up the blanket and put on my bathing suit while he dressed. Then we crawled back out from the hedge. Werner asked me if we could meet again tomorrow. I told him I was not sure and I would try my best. We kissed again then went our separate ways. I waited a few minutes for him to cycle off before emerging from the trees and making my way to the kindergarten and home.

When I arrived home I had a wash for obvious reasons. I could not sit across the dinner table from Joachim with another man's semen trickling out of me. In fact I sat and wondered to myself just how many other women had experienced this same predicament as me. It was at that point I realised that we had been stupid and had not used any form of contraception. As I prepared the evening meal I thought about this constantly. Yet at the same time I wanted more. When Joachim arrived home he kissed me on the cheek and sat down at the table. We both ate dinner in relative silence before the howl of an air raid siren began. This was the first time I ever recall hearing it. We both looked at each other like startled cats. Joachim mumbled, "Fucking hell, it can't be." I ran upstairs and grabbed Roel from his bed, ran back down the stairs and we both dragged the heavy kitchen table to the alcove in the wall and we got down underneath it. We did not have a shelter out the back at that time. We never thought it necessary. We waited and heard the distant drone of aircraft. There were a few flak explosions, which seemed distant too. Roel did not seem alarmed by this intrusion into his sleep and was soon fast asleep again. After less than an hour the all clear was given and we crawled out from under the table. We looked at one another and laughed and then we began kissing. I quickly put Roel back to bed then went back down to the kitchen. Me and Joachim made passionate love there and then on the kitchen floor. It was the end of a really weird yet exciting day, all for the wrong reasons. My parents would have been horrified beyond belief had they known what I'd done. It seems I am trapped between two different worlds here, unsure of what I am going to do. I wanted to spend time with Werner yet loved but was not in love with Joachim anymore. It makes no sense, I know, yet I can only write it down here for what use it will ever be.

Lisa Schauer, her parents, two younger brothers, Friedrich and Alfred, and younger sister, Ursula, lived in the eastern sector of the municipality of Unterhaching, in Munich. Lisa was nineteen years of age in 1941. She divided her time between working in one of the town's small cafés and helping her grandparents. Lisa still recalls many experiences under the Third Reich, some amusing, and some extremely sinister:

I spent lots of time at my grandparents as I loved them dearly. I used to stay and sleep at their home any time I could. I loved their home as everything was so old. They had a huge open fire, lots of old brassware and old wooden beams ran across the ceilings of every room in their house. Their garden was beautiful in summer. It was packed with fragrant flowers. Both my grandparents loved their garden as many old people did and still do.

One thing I can vividly recall of our lives […] was the gypsy people who often came by our grandparent's home. I always found them slightly scary and my grandmother used to warn me that if they came I should run inside. As a younger child, this caused me to question why I should do this. My grandmother would tell me that the gypsy people would think nothing of kidnapping me and putting me in a big, black box in the back of one of their wagons. I think this came about as a result of the National Socialists after the defeat of 1918. My parents and grandparents thought the Nazis were our saviours so naturally we were persuaded likewise as they were our elders and knew better than us. Grandmother and grandfather would sit me on their knees as a little girl and tell me of the post-1918 years when many Germans lived in poverty while greedy Weimar politicians and wealthy Jews prospered on our agony. They were strong stories for young ears but I believed them. They used to say that whole families perished in the winters and many others starved.

The gypsy people had already been largely ostracised and it was not safe for them in many parts of Germany. The gypsy people who came by my grandparents' home probably slipped across from Poland or somewhere, I don't know. They would often pull up in a horse-drawn caravan, which was very colourful and decorative. An old gypsy lady would offer to tell our fortunes for us, either for money or an exchange of goods. I can remember one morning a horse-drawn wagon pulling up and a young gypsy man jumped from the front of his wagon and began to admire my grandmother's roses in her garden. He learned forward to smell one, cupping it in his hands. All of a sudden my grandmother flung open her windows and shouted at him, "What are you doing there? You look like a rat!" The man had a dark, tanned face and characteristically leathery-looking skin […]. Yes, they did look different to us Germans and were not welcomed in many cases. When my grandmother shouted the man just slowly looked up and held his hands up in the air and then asked if we had some water for his horse. My grandmother told him, "There is nothing for you here. Now go away or I will fetch a gun to you." By this time the man's family appeared wearily from the back of their wagon. Three little children in all, two girls and a boy, stood, stretching their arms and legs out on the dusty road. No sooner had they got out than their father was shouting for them to get back in again. They then drove off up the lane.

On my way back home later I was walking and saw the gypsy family parked up in a field not far from my grandparents' house. My curiosity made me stand and stare at them from the fence. They saw me standing watching them and one of the children, a boy, ran across to me. For a minute we just stared at one another awkwardly. Then he asked me if I would like to come and stroke the horse. I told him I couldn't as I was told that gypsies took young children away from their homes and that they were dangerous. The boy's father then appeared and told me if I wanted to stroke the horses that they would do me no harm. "We are travelling people and go where the wind takes us," he said with a broad smile on what looked an ancient face. I climbed the fence and dropped down into the grassy field and walked with them to their wagon. A fire was burning and a pot hung beneath a kind of stand made with tree branches. I peered into it and there were potatoes and other summer vegetables bubbling away in it with what looked like rabbit meat. I apprehensively peeked in through the door of their wagon. There was a young woman and an old woman in there, the man's wife and mother, so he said. The inside of the wagon was meticulously clean with what looked like tapestries hanging inside. The old lady was working on one right at that moment. They smiled and said hello and not to be afraid of them as they wouldn't hurt anyone. The children ran around in the long grass playing chase and they just seemed every bit as normal as us, not the scroungers or thieves as portrayed by the Nazis. I […] found myself running around playing chase with the gypsy children. I was nine years old at the time and maybe I should have just gone straight home.

The next thing, I heard the voice of my father roaring across the field from the gate, "Lisa! Come here now this instant, you stupid child!" I turned and immediately ran to my father. When I climbed back over the fence my white dress had dirt on it and he was furious with me. He struck me hard there and then and shouted at me, "How dare you do this. What have these vagabonds been saying and doing with you?" I tried to tell him that it was alright, I had just stroked the horse, said hello and was playing a game with the children. He grabbed my arm and pulled me along, but not after stopping to warn the gypsy family that he was reporting the incident to the local police. I began to cry as I knew I was in big trouble and those people would also be in big trouble too. When we got home my father removed his belt from his trousers and hit me across the bottom. Mother was furious too and after the beating I was sent to my room, where I was told to read the bible. My grandparents were told and they came to visit a few days later. They told me off, too, and said I could never go to their home and stay again if I could not be trusted to behave as a German girl should behave. Of course, I did go again, but was always walked home afterwards by one of the local men who was a friend of my parents.

I remember when we walked by the field where, just a few weeks previously, I had been playing with the gypsy people. There was a pile of blackened, burnt wood and the rotting remains of a horse. I wanted to stop to look but was pulled away by the arm. The authorities […] had arrested the gypsies, killed their horse and set alight to their wagon. Their crime […] was trying to kidnap a German girl. The locals all knew and would say to me, "We heard you were rescued just in time by your brave father, but don't worry, they will all be dealt with soon." Of course, it was all a lie. They had never harmed or intended to harm me. It was a fabrication by the authorities.

I soon learned after that, and through my school years, that we were to have nothing to do with these people. They were looked upon as a race of vermin and despised as much as Jews. We were shown films and things, so by the time I was in my teens and early twenties, I too was convinced they were bad people. They and the Jews were rightfully being erased from our country and the territories we occupied as Germans. I used to believe I had a lucky escape. Only now do I look back and think how stupid I was to believe it all. They were no more a menace to me than anyone else, yet there would be a concerted effort to wipe them all out pretty soon. We had created this heaven for the Germanic people where no other races were permitted to live among us. Yet it was a view of heaven through a bullet hole for many of us.

Chapter 5

What the Devil Brings

By May of 1941 Kitka Obermann was helplessly embroiled in an affair with the young Werner Bothe, who she had met and befriended during the previous summer months. The two had swapped their meetings in the local park on sunny days for visits to Werner's home while his parents were away on business. The couple would often go the house, where their time would be divided between talking about the future and making love. It was in the June of that year that Kitka discovered, to her horror, that she was pregnant. She recalls:

> I got up the one morning and felt dreadfully sick. I vomited several times over the course of the day and just thought that maybe I had contracted something. It never initially occurred to me that I was pregnant. I hadn't made love with Joachim for some time. In fact we had not made love for six months. The only man that had taken that pleasure of me was Werner. Me and Joachim had continued to drift apart as he became more absorbed than ever in his work. I had stupidly not insisted on using birth control every time when making love with Werner. We had been so overcome with the excitement of it all. Besides, it felt so much nicer without him having one of those rubber things stuck on it. It was only after visiting my doctor that I was told, "Congratulations, fräulein, you are not ill, you are expecting a child." The doctor's words came as an unpleasant shock to me. He could see the horror in my facial expression and asked if there was anything wrong. I got up and told him, "No. I am fine. I am just tired that's all."
>
> I caught the tram home, feeling terribly scared of what I was going to do now. I could not turn to my parents as they

would have gone mad at me. We did not get on well as it was. Breaking the news to Joachim was the question. He knew very well that if I were pregnant the chances were the baby was not going to be his. God, what a mess I have created, I thought to myself. I could not have this child without Joachim or my family discovering it. My only real option was to tell the truth. I would have to tell Joachim, hard as that was going to be. I was frightened of how he might react. Would he beat me and throw me out of the house? Where would I go if this happened? Would young Werner cut off all of his interest in me now I was expecting his child? The questions rolled about inside my mind. As I travelled home on the tram my immediate world was a mixture of delirium and white noise. It was as if I was trapped in some alternate place within my mind. A goldfish bowl from which there could be no escape. I got off the tram and collected Roel from school. He came running out waving a small swastika flag in his hand. He had been learning the basics of National Socialism for young children. As we walked home my mind was in complete turmoil. I felt like breaking down and crying but I knew I couldn't.

It was later that evening that I broke the news of my affair to Joachim. He was sat there as usual with his nose in a newspaper. We had just cleared the dinner things away. I stood alone at the sink, washing up, trying to build myself up to tell him. I just said, "Joachim, I have something to tell you and you are going to hate me for it and you may even want to kill me for it. I can't keep this from you any longer. I know we have grown apart over the past year and this has caused a problem." He dropped his newspaper down and looked at me, puzzled. He replied, "What are you trying to say to me, Katherine? All I have ever done is try and provide for you and our son. Now what are you going on about?" I just blurted it out, "I am pregnant, but with another man's child." At that point his whole composure left him, "What the fucking hell do you mean, another man's child? Are you trying to tell me you have been fucking someone else behind my back, Katherine?" I told him "yes" and just broke down in tears. He sat in silence as I wept, for what must have ten long minutes. I could tell how much my words had hurt him. He then told me, "You had better go to your mother and father's. I don't want you here. I will take our son to my sister's and she will take care of him until I decide what I am going to do about this. I don't want to see your face here again. If I need to speak to you, I will ask my sister to visit you at your parents', or she will write to you with instructions." I begged him not to take Roel away from me as I needed him. He just shouted at me, "Get out of here now. This is what becomes of any married woman who chooses to become another man's whore."

It was the first time I had sensed that violence could erupt. I ran upstairs, grabbed a few things and left the house. I would have no choice but to either return home or go to my brother's house, which would take me two hours to walk. As I left the house that had been our home I felt like a car that had just been in a crash. I sobbed as I walked in the dark to my brother's home. Two soldiers stopped me and asked me if I was alright. I told them I was okay, that I just needed to get to my brother's house. They offered me a ride and I accepted. They told me, "Whatever it is, fräulein, it will pass." They guessed I must have had a row with my boyfriend or husband. If they had known would they have treated me any differently? The two soldiers dropped me off and, like true gentlemen, they escorted me to the front door of my brother's house. My brother was visibly shocked to see me and in such an emotional state. He was very concerned and quickly helped me inside and made me a hot drink. His wife, bless her, wrapped a blanket around me even though it was summer. I felt chilled to the bone and was trembling due to the experiences of the past few hours. My brother and his wife made me comfortable and then asked what had happened. I had to sit there and explain in all the sordid details of what I had done. After explaining myself my brother showed me to the spare room. I could stay with them for the time being until things were sorted out. I didn't sleep that night at all. I thought of Roel, my parents, what I was going to do, and the need to contact Werner as soon as possible.

A couple of nights later I was again lying awake, just staring at the ceiling. I heard a commotion outside and got up and carefully parted the curtains. I saw a group of men outside the house opposite my brother's home. With their leather coats and black hats I knew straight away these men were the secret police or the Gestapo. It was three in the morning and they were banging on the door of the house. Some of them went around the back. When the door opened the men burst in and the door slammed shut behind them. A few minutes later five people were bundled outside and into three separate cars. The doors of the cars slammed shut and they sped off down the road. At breakfast later that morning my brother told me, "The Leuschner family had been under suspicion of hiding Jews in their basement. Two Jews were indeed found in the basement of their home and all were arrested." My brother then just laughed and said, "Hiding bloody Jews in our neighbourhood of all places. Those traitors deserve all that they get now." I later heard that the Leuschner family, who I never knew but were known to my brother and were thought of as good Germans, had been sent to one of the camps. That's what they were referred to back then, simply as camps. From what I knew at the time if you went into one of these camps the chances were you would never be heard from again. Later on that day, in the afternoon, I made contact with Werner. He had been worried sick as he had been looking out for me at our meeting place for the last three days. When I told him what had happened he just looked at me, smiled reassuringly and held my hand, saying, "Does this mean you are mine now, my beautiful dear Kitka?"

The whole course of the Second World War was to change drastically for Germany on Sunday, 22 June 1941. Germany's ambitions towards Russia and the east had been no secret amongst the higher echelons of the German military. The conquest of the east, primarily for *Lebensraum*

(Living Space), had been one of Hitler's greatest desires for many years prior to the actual attempt at invading Soviet Russia. He had made a non-aggression pact with Stalin and maybe the Russian leader had been naïve enough to believe Hitler would honour the agreement. The warnings were there for the Soviets well before the actual attack came, yet Stalin believed that any talk of a German invasion of Russia was purely fabrication on the part of Britain and an attempt to sabotage German-Russian relations. When the invasion did start, on 22 June, it came as a complete shock to the Russians, but it was to prove Hitler's most catastrophic folly yet.

Russia has faced invasion countless times in her history but has never been successfully invaded by any modern army. Some have occupied areas of her territory and enslaved her people, yet these occupations have often been relatively short lived affairs due to the sheer tenacity and natural resourcefulness of the Russian people. Hitler had gambled on a fast-moving campaign of aircraft, tanks, artillery and infantry, hoping to secure victory before the Russian winter set in. It was a hugely ambitious plan and few of his Generals were optimistic of success. But though they could see the danger in Hitler's planning, none were brave enough to argue with the Führer himself.

Initially the German invasion went better than many of the Generals had expected. Many thousands of Russian soldiers were killed, forced to surrender or taken prisoner. As the German *Blitzkrieg* rolled through Russia the security divisions followed. These units were primarily concerned with the mopping up process in the wake of the regular forces, ensuring no attacks were made on the German rear. Soon stories of whole villages being wiped out by the SS and the security divisions began to filter out. Germany's war in the east would become one of the most brutal, barbaric campaigns in military history. For the time being many Germans, particularly the young, were complacent as to the impending dangers. As hundreds of young German families were sent to colonise the newly conquered territories in the east, a new euphoria took hold. In German cities propaganda proclaimed that only 'apes' had previously inhabited the eastern territories. These 'apes' would be systematically erased and replaced with Germanic stock. As the Russians were sent fleeing in the face of the initial German onslaught, back home many Germans celebrated – prematurely – a great victory over the hated Soviets.

Ursula Bomme recalled:

There was no question of any sense of danger at the time regarding our invasion of Russia. The advances being made by our military were rapid and it was said Moscow would soon be captured and our flags would be flying over the city. We had no reason to think otherwise. Even though Britain had still to be dealt with it was classed as nothing more than an irritation that could wait. I remember at school; the Russians, we were told, were nothing. Our teacher would say, "These people of the east are not intelligent, merely apes, sub-human. We can exist alongside them only temporarily until the Führer's will dictates otherwise." He was in a sense hinting at the fact that war was likely between us and Russia, even though our leadership were friendly towards one another at that time. In that June of 1941 the non-aggression treaty was in tatters; we had another enemy to face and a war now on two fronts. Still, at that time we especially at home sensed no danger. We were convinced Russia would fall before winter.

Helena Koerg's father arrived the Sunday after the news of the invasion of Russia had broken. She recalled how he sat silently, deep in his own thoughts, for most of the morning:

He barely said a word and appeared unhappy. I sat down beside him and holding his hand I said to him, "Father, are you thinking of dear Peter?" He replied, "Yes I am, and I can think of nothing else. My boy has no grave, we have nothing we can go and place flowers on for your dear brother. He lies at the bottom of the sea somewhere. This business with Russia, I hope Hitler knows what he has got us all into." "What do you mean, father?' I asked? "Well, it takes little thought, does it not? Napoleon embarked on Russia and was soundly defeated. I have a very uneasy feeling about all of this. Our enemies surround us and I am frightened of the future, we all should be." I tried to reassure father and advised him to not speak like this as he might get into trouble if he were ever heard. We both sat there and had a cry, and I from the corner of my eye I saw my mother stop the girls from entering the room. She sent them out into the garden and then peered around the door and said, "You two must compose yourself, especially around the girls. We all have to be strong as they are still missing their uncle Peter terribly." We dried our tears and I joined mother back in the kitchen.

Gertrud Koerg also remembers that day and her grandpapa's apprehensive mood:

I went and sat down with him after dinner while the others were in the garden. I remember saying to him, "We are conquering apes, not men, in Russia, grandpapa. We have the greatest army in the world and we will win." I remember grandpapa just looking up at me from his chair and saying, "The Soviets may be apes in the eyes of the government. Make no mistake, they are a cunning enemy; a tough, resilient people used to living with very little and fighting with no food in their stomachs in conditions we might call atrocious. That is the difference with the Russians. No army has ever defeated Russia. What makes ours any different to the others who have tried and failed?" I said to grandpapa, "You can't speak like that," to which he replied, "And you can't speak like that as a young girl. Forget all this nonsense." I knew what he meant and as he got up from his chair he cuddled me close to him, and then we went out into the garden to join the others.

The older generation were rightfully anxious about Hitler's war in the east while the young were convinced that this was Germany fulfilling one of its greatest goals. Throughout the summer of 1941 the German army, in combination with the Luftwaffe, made remarkable progress. Yet, with the German failure to capture Moscow, all notions of a quick victory soon began to evaporate. As the winter of 1941 approached it also occurred to the German commanders in the field that their forces still had no supplies of winter clothing. It was also a cruel irony that the winter of 1941 would be one of the worst on record. The temperatures fluctuated between -10°C to lows of -50°C. With wind-chill factors taken into consideration the conditions were horrific. Snow and ice added to the problems faced by the German forces. Many German soldiers huddled in freezing trenches on the Eastern Front would pray for the warm salvation of death.

It was around this time during the Second World War that the German home front first began to mobilise. The idea started with women and girls forming groups to knit and make clothing which would then be sent to the beleaguered German forces. Gertrud Koerg recalled how her *Jungmadelbund* troop was encouraged to help the German soldiers in Russia. She recalled:

> It began with a long speech from our leader about how a nation helps its own and a true patriot will carry out any duty he or she is asked. She then asked the question "How many girls present here today can knit?" A few hands went up, including mine. My grandmother had taught me knitting through the past winters. I often made baby clothes for friends and relatives so I knew I could do it. The leader looked around and ordered all the girls who could not knit to learn with immediate effect. In fact, she said, "You can start to learn this instant." So we who could knit paired up with a girl who could not and began to teach them. I was a patient teacher [...]. Other girls were not so patient and I heard them grumbling things like "Oh god, not again. You don't do it like that, you do it like this!" It must have been frustrating for those who had never picked up knitting needles. I heard one of my friends say, "This knitting is for old women not young girls," to which another girl retorted, "Try saying that to your dear brother when he is in Russia dying from the cold."

The nation was expected to rally to the cry for warm clothing to be sent east, yet Hitler's policy of clothes rationing meant that few Germans, apart from the wealthy, had spare clothes to donate. However, any who claimed they had nothing to donate were reminded that the German army was in far greater need of warm clothing than civilians at home. Groups of women would get together and sort through their husbands', sons' and brothers' clothing selecting any that might provide some extra warmth to a German soldier fighting in the east. Helena Koerg recalled:

> We formed knitting groups with our friends, which was the easiest method at the time. There was plenty of wool and many women and girls were able to knit and make jumpers, gloves, socks, hats and scarves. The skills of the women varied; some were very good at knitting while others were pretty terrible at it. The old women would work very fast and complete their pieces of clothing way before the others, wearing a smug grin on their faces. These meetings were often like a church coffee morning without the coffee. Either way we worked hard as one piece of clothing was completed another was started straight away. I heard one woman say after a few weeks of this labour, "We have made all this lovely clothing, now how are they going to get this stuff out there to our men in Russia?" Her remark was met with the shrugging of shoulders and blank faces. No one said anything as I doubt anyone had really thought about that.

Whilst the German offensive was brought to a standstill by the severe winter conditions Germans back home continued their support. The items of clothing donated or made by the women and girls of Germany was collected and then flown out to the troops at the various battlefronts. Supplying the German armies in the east had become something of a logistical nightmare, especially during the winter months. Snow storms, fog and other bad weather would prevent Luftwaffe supply drops from taking place. The reality was that there had been little to no contingency planning for the conditions the German forces were now battling against. Winter would become as much an enemy as the Russians themselves. Furthermore, the sheer scale of the Eastern Front campaign had been over ambitious and the resilience of the enemy underestimated. There were, of course, successes, but the turning point of the Second World War was fast approaching as opportunities slipped from Germany's grasp.

As Christmas of 1941 loomed concerns about the war were soon at the back of most people's minds. At this stage there were no food shortages and civilian life continued much as normal, despite the RAF raids that were taking place. Many Germans at home were looking forward to Christmas. Those women with husbands, sons and brothers away fighting would be busily preparing parcels for their loved ones. These Christmas parcels contained gift items such as letters, photographs and greeting cards, rings, pendants, cigarettes, lighters, cakes, sweets and, of course, items of warm clothing. The parcels were checked to ensure they contained no contraband items and letters were read to ensure they contained nothing that may have a detrimental effect upon the soldier's morale. Many Germans were 'doing okay', as they put it, but this would change on Sunday, 7 December 1941, when the Japanese (Germany's Axis ally) attacked United States Navy ships anchored at Pearl Harbor in Hawaii. Gertrud Koerg remembers hearing news of the attack:

> I first heard about it during the evening of Sunday, 7 December. I had not long had a bath in front of the fire in our living area. I went upstairs and put on my nightgown and some wool socks because it was very cold and we had no heating upstairs back in those days. A friend of my father's came round and said that the Japanese had attacked the Americans in Hawaii and had inflicted grave losses. He was babbling about the whole of the American Pacific fleet being destroyed. My father said, "Yes, but is all of this true? Have you got your information correct?" He just kept saying "Yes, it's all true." I had come down the stairs and sat cuddling with my mother while my father and his friend talked. Before long there were more knocks at the door as other neighbours came to see if we had heard the news. Everybody tuned on their radio sets to see if there was any news on the attack. It was difficult to tell propaganda from truth in the immediate aftermath of the attack, but over the days that followed we were told about it at school, at the *Jungmadelbund* meeting and, of course, it was all over our newspapers, so we knew it was true.

When news of the Japanese attack on Pearl Harbor reached Adolf Hitler he was said to have been ecstatic, even though the Japanese had not confided with their German ally. Hitler was unconcerned and boasted, 'We can't lose the war at all. We now have an ally which has never been conquered in three thousand years.' Although Hitler hinted that a day would come when Germany would have to fight a war against Japan, for the time being the Führer was happy to hear good news. Many Germans shared his enthusiasm, but the jubilation would be short lived. On 11 December 1941 the United States of America declared war against the Empire of Japan and her Axis allies, Germany and Italy. Many Germans had been relatively unconcerned by the war with Britain, but they fully understood that America's entry into the war would change everything. The industrial might of the USA, coupled with her manpower capabilities, would prove the proverbial nail in the coffin for Germany in the Second World War.

On learning of the American declaration of war against Germany, Helena Koerg felt genuine fear for the first time:

> I understood that it was just a matter of time now before America would gain her strength and mobilize against us. I had visited America as a young girl. I had seen how well developed it was as an industrial power. America could make thousands of cars a day. America would soon be building a thousand tanks, aeroplanes and artillery guns a day. All that would be hurled against us. I felt fearful for my family […]. What would we do if bigger air attacks came, if food became in very short supply and if we could find no fuel for our fires in winter? What if our soldiers lost the war in the East, our Luftwaffe lost the war in the air? It was all a case of what if. I was very scared on hearing of America's entry into the war. My father was even more depressed. He swore about Hitler, using a word I cannot repeat here. He said, "We have the whole world against us. It will be as much as we can do to survive all of this. We are going to have to plan, grow more vegetables and learn to live off as little as we can. This is all going to get very nasty." I kept quiet and told Reinhard not to say anything that would frighten the girls.
>
> On my father's advice the following weekend we began to prepare an air raid shelter in the back garden. We all helped dig it out. Father insisted, "Dig it as deep as you can and as far back from the house as you can as your lives may well depend on it." We dug it out up against the red brick

wall which was at the bottom of our garden. It was sheltered by some fruit trees which would help protect against bomb splinters. Heavy wooden boarding was set in along the sides reinforced with corrugated metal sheeting. Then once all the wood and metal was in place we covered it with soil. Sandbags were also placed around the shelter, and in all it was pretty big and we felt it would be reasonably comfortable inside. My father built a wooden door for it and then a heavy wool blanket was hung in front of this door to help keep any cold draughts out. People used to come and see our shelter and they would say, "Helena, Reinhard, you have the best shelter in this whole street!" Then I recall this one woman's thirteen-year-old daughter pushing through and looking at the shelter. Shaking her head, she said, "Very good, but if a bomb lands directly on top of this you will all die." The girl's mother grabbed her by the arm and said, "Sasha, don't talk like that." The girl pulled a face and walked away. I think Gertrud knew her from the Jungmadelbund. I didn't like her at all as she was a horrible spoiled brat.

Gertrud recalls:

I knew Sasha Goelinger very well. She was twelve, the same age as me, went to the same school and was also in my *Jungmadelbund* group. She was always writing letters and cards to our soldiers. So much so our teachers at school suggested we should follow her example and write a letter or card each and every day for a German soldier fighting in Russia. As she grew older the content of her letters became quite explicit. Sasha was also good at pencil sketching. She often sketched explicit sexual scenes. She once sketched the Führer having sex with a beautiful girl [she laughs]. She often read her letters out to me before she posted them. She would laugh about them as she ran the tip of her tongue across the gummed line of the envelope before sealing it. Some of her letters were later returned and she received a warning about their sexual content and how it might distract a soldier from his duties. Sasha always made jokes about this. She once told me, "Well, I think it's a good thing, Gertrud. If they are thinking about coming home and the possibility of fucking me stupid on my bed, they won't be thinking anything negative such as dying or being captured, will they?" I was shocked by her comment, yet Sasha was an odd girl for sure. Mother didn't like her as she thought she was a brat, and that she had everything she wanted.

Christmas 1941 passed relatively peacefully in Germany. As the snows came the people celebrated. It was really difficult to imagine at this point that just four short years later much of the country would lie in ruin and millions would be dead. Helena Koerg sat down on Christmas Eve 1941 and wrote the following in her diary:

This year has not been as hard on us as it has for some in Germany. We lost my dear brother, Peter, in March. It has hit mother and father so terribly hard and Gertrud still cries at night sometimes as I have heard her. There is nothing at all we can do yet I still hope that someday he will return home and walk through the door, and that this would all have been some kind of nightmare […] I run up, throw my arms around him, and say, "Oh, brother, they told me you were dead, missing somewhere in the sea." He would be shaking his head and saying, "No, don't be so silly." But then I would wake up and cry like a child. Me and Reinhard will make this Christmas as good as we can for our daughters. We have a few presents and we have food, and mother and father will join us, as they always do. Please, all I ask dear God is that this war business ends very soon before more people suffer and more die. The world will not forgive Germany lightly this time. This war maybe one too many, we just don't know. We must hold our breath and see what the devil brings.

Chapter 6

A Haunting Picture

Hilde Hermann was a nineteen-year-old university student from Berlin. In April 1942 she received notice requiring her to report for a medical examination prior to her obligatory *Landjahr* (country service year). Hilde recalls:

> I had been interested in human biology for many years. It was a subject which fascinated me and I enjoyed it very much. I wanted a profession in human biology and studied the subject at university. The problem was back then if you were a university student you were regarded very highly and they expected so much more from you. It was more or less compulsory to do the country service year. Had I refused to carry out my *Landjahr* then I could not have graduated. It was as simple as that so I had no choice really. I received a letter informing me of the details of my Landjahr and a medical I would have to attend prior to leaving home.
>
> I had no worries about the medical examination. I was as fit as I could possibly be and participated in all manner of sports activities. In fact, sports and exercise had figured prominently in my life over the past ten or so years. My family were active in sports and we all had to join in. Then there was the *Jungmadelbund* and *Bund Deutscher Madel*, who exploited sporting activities to the limit. I was in my prime in the eyes of our authorities. I knew from my biology teachings the principles of Aryanism, race and eugenics. I had learned all about that and its application to the Nazi German view of human biology.
>
> The medical examination was like many I had already been through over the years. The examiners loved the

blonde-haired, blue-eyed, athletic young women. You would see their eyes light up when you walked into the room. They were eager to get your clothes off and start measuring you up and looking at the shape of your face, ears and nose. If you had the Aryan look you were a prize specimen [she laughs]. People often ask me, "How did you feel being measured and prodded and touched like a prize cow or something?" I would say it never bothered me at all. Among the other girls we were encouraged to be naturally beautiful in the sense that we could not wear makeup or perfume. We were raised to not be shy of our bodies or being naked in front of others, even the men. Being naked was not construed as being lustful. Sex and nakedness were two different functions. In our book, as we used to say, nakedness was a celebration of the perfect German female [or male] form. Sex was the lustful occupation of lesser races and their pursuit of gratification and pleasure. Our sex was purely to produce more strong and obedient German children. It was not seen as an act of pleasure you understand.

As I stood naked throughout my examination with my hands on my hips I knew what was going through the minds of the male doctors examining me. However much they preached this guff about studying Aryanism and things I knew full well they were thinking how much they would like to fuck me. Their hands were cold and clammy, and trembled with excitement. Their long, white coats hid what must have been aching erections. They took photographs, and if all was well they would sign you over as fit for your Landjahr. I didn't mind having to do Landjahr service, but I would have rather spent nine months working on my biology studies than on a farm somewhere. When my Landjahr began I was one of thirty-five young women going on what was termed a "special placement in the East". After Poland had been crushed and the invasion of Soviet Russia had begun the authorities were keen to Germanize certain areas of these conquered territories. The idea was to exploit the new territories for resources, which could then be used by the Reich.

We were billeted on a large farm a few miles outside Warsaw. The farm looked a mess to me, with rundown buildings and lots of mud. It was not the picturesque scene I had imagined it would be. We arrived on the Saturday; our sleeping quarters were arranged and we began work on the Monday morning. The people who had been appointed as being in charge of this farm were, of course, German farmers who had been relocated here to oversee the running of the place. They were hardly the peasant types that many of the Poles were; they were well-fed, strong and fit and demanded Nazi salutes. We were used to all of that so it was not a problem.

The work was extremely tough and unpleasant and I began to hate it. Of course, keeping one's mouth shut was a priority. You did not moan or complain […] for fear of getting into trouble. You had to just get on with it. I spent days helping to repair fencing, shovelling shit here and there, helping with the chickens and pigs and other animals. At the close of each day the animals had to be checked and fed before we could go and wash and have our evening meal. You felt so tired sometimes that you didn't feel like washing, but we could never go to bed smelling like pigs, could we? We would wash and change and then we all sat down together to eat. The farmer in charge and his family kept a close eye on everyone and noted each individual's aptitude for work and how well they performed. In a very short time most of the hard work was done and it got a little easier.

As the summer of 1942 got closer we felt the warmth of the sun. There was a huge lake not far away and we were permitted to swim there, under supervision of course. When we swam we did so naked. None of us had bathing suits or hats. That fresh water was bone chilling, even in the summer months. It was nice to climb out and just sit on the bank and let the sunshine warm you through. Photographers were always coming to take pictures of us. These photographs were used for propaganda in various Nazi periodicals and Hitler Youth yearbooks too. We sometimes asked for copies which we would then send to our parents in letters. This was very common at that stage of the war. Things were not too bad at that time and, yes, it was hard work, but we had some fun too. A film crew arrived one morning while we were working in the hayfields. The film guys stayed around for a few hours, asking us to do certain things so they could film us. The film had been specially commissioned by the Reich propaganda ministry, so we were told. It didn't occur to me that they had gathered only the tall, blonde-haired, Aryan-looking girls together for this piece of film. I felt sorry for the others who had to stand behind the camera and watch.

When the cereal crops were ready for harvesting the finished grain product was then transported back to Germany, along with vegetables of all kinds. Even the pigs and chickens were slaughtered and the meat cured and sent back to Germany. They used to say "supplying the home front, feeding our families and our soldiers within Germany itself is paramount to our activities here." The Poles got very little in comparison. We didn't have much contact with the Poles to be honest. If we went out anywhere we went as a group and we had people with us to keep an eye out on us all. Poles were pushed out of our way if we were walking up a road somewhere and told "get out of here". I recall once we had encountered some Polish men walking towards us. They were swiftly told to "get out of our way" and to "move over to the other side of the road". We felt like Roman legionnaires or something. The Poles moved, as instructed, to the other side and stood with their heads bowed as we passed them. I heard fighting near the back and when I looked these Polish men were being set about by men who had been shadowing us from a distance. My friend said they were the Hitler Youth police or something. I asked, "What do you think they are doing?" She replied, "I am not sure, Hilde, but maybe it is best we don't ask too many questions."

It was a Sunday afternoon and we often had games and competitions on weekends. We could win prizes and gifts of various kinds so we enjoyed it. There was one place I remember vividly and it was not long before my time was

finished and I returned home to Germany. It was a small
[…] cemetery for German soldiers who had been killed in
the invasion. We would go there every weekend and make
sure it was clean and tidy and we had to put fresh flowers on
all the graves there. Again, there were often photographers
there taking pictures of us. I quite liked going there but felt
sadness that these boys were so far from home that their
families could not possibly visit as often as they would like.
Before I left to go home to my family and finish university
I heard some Polish men had been caught looting some of
the graves, looking for any valuables they might then sell.
They were caught in the act and I heard they were all hung
from a tree outside the cemetery as warning to any other
would-be looters. It made me feel ill. On the train home we
stopped off a few times. We even passed a consignment of
Jews on their way to the east. Their destination was unknown
to us yet their plight reminded me of helpless animals en
route to the slaughterhouse.

Having completed my Landjahr I graduated from
university and had hoped to work in a medical context in
one of the hospitals. Initially they tried to dissuade me from
taking on a career and sat me down telling me I could do
this or do that. I was even once offered a placement in an
asylum as a junior. I soon discovered that in these asylums
they were not caring for people but were murdering them.
Sadly it appears that many of the patients were killed with
the consent of their families. The families would sign them
over to the authorities who then killed them under the Aktion
T4 euthanasia programme. I could not be a part of that, even
though the pay I was offered was great. In the end I was
finally granted a laboratory job in the pathology department
of the local hospital.

The atmosphere in our country was changing steadily at
this time. Before the war our government had been trying
to persuade women that we would best be serving the
Reich as wives at home. There was this prejudice towards
women being equal to the men and being self-sufficient as
individuals. They didn't want that to evolve and I had to

really work hard to convince them that I could contribute better working in the clinical field as opposed to being a homemaker. I had to bluff them and tell them my work would be for the greater good of our people. I was then moved to another place where I was given human brains to examine. The brains were inside clear jars filled with a clear solution to preserve them. They would be taken out of the jars and examined for any anomalies. I was informed later that many of the brains had been taken from the corpses of concentration camp prisoners, or the criminally insane and the mentally ill. Of particular interest to those commissioning the research were the brains of eastern Europeans. These brains were compared to the brains of healthy Germans who had donated organs specifically for research purposes. I sensed that there was something very sinister about all of this work. For what purpose was it all to serve? My parents just told me to "do your study work and ask no questions."

Kitka Obermann had suffered greatly for her romantic liaisons with her lover, Werner Bothe. After discovering she was pregnant with Werner's child she was compelled to reveal the affair to her husband, Joachim. After her last diary entry there appeared a gap of almost eight months. Her son, Roel, could shine no light on what happened to his mother during this time. He said she would never discuss it. Roel recalls that he and his mother went to stay with her brother then ended up at his grandparents' home. It was not a favourable arrangement and Roel recalls many heated arguments. As a child, Roel understood little of the turmoil going on around him. Due to various problems, he had lived for a short time with an aunt before being handed back to his mother. The intervention of the local authorities also helped his mother's case. He missed his father although his mother took him to visit regularly and never denied his father access to his son. Roel recalls:

I remember my mother taking me to our old home some months after my parents' separation. On this one occasion my father took me to where he worked. One of the things I recall from that visit to the Dornier works was when they were testing an engine for one of the bombers. It was the loudest thing I had ever heard as the big BMW radial spluttered into life. I recall the look of pride on my father's face as the engine was signed off for fitting. Then he took me to a sub-assembly line where parts were put together. When I think back I can see how obsessed my father was with his work. Of course I knew he loved me, and still loved my mother. I understood later on why mother did what she did. She married and had me very young; too young really. She became bored and irritated with her life. It was not an easy time though and in some ways we all suffered separately. My mother clashed with her parents all the time. I remember them shouting things at her like "You stupid, useless girl". Of course, they were my grandparents and so I was piggy in the middle of all of this fighting.

The first time I met the father of my future little brother I was amazed at how youthful he appeared, and the vast home he lived in. To me he was this strange man we were now going to live with. To be totally honest he was a good man. He obviously adored my mother so much. He would never let her do anything menial, he would always do it for her. He was always buying her things and he often bought me nice toys as well. We went to live at his home with his parents and we had part of their house to ourselves. They were concerned about their son living with another man's wife and young child, but my mother was pregnant with a child who would be their grandchild. Things settled down and my mother and father agreed to divorce. It was not the done thing back then to divorce and I know mother had a lot of trouble from the other local women. They would treat her as if she was a harlot or something. It was something I just had to get used to until I was older and able to defend her against those bullies.

When Kitka began writing in her journal again she wrote the following:

My life has been a whirlwind of emotions over the past months. Living with mother and father was, as I expected, a nightmare which did neither me nor Roel any good at all. I thank God that Werner was not like many of the boys you encounter today. He loves me and wants to spend as much time as he can with me and Roel. He is a good man and now when I go to the park Werner comes with me. We are like a family again even though things have changed forever. Mother and father rarely talk to me. They are interested only in Roel and refuse to have Werner in their house. I have written to them, but it makes no difference. The Zeppelin factory has been bombed and I fear this is just the start. Our soldiers in Russia are struggling with an enemy who is proving far more stubborn than expected.

By Christmas of 1942 Germany was in its third year of war. Any notion of a quick victory was, by this stage, completely dispelled. The *Wehrmacht* had its nose badly blooded in the east. Both they and the Luftwaffe were suffering heavy casualties and as a result more men were encouraged to enlist for military service. Badly wounded soldiers who were repatriated back to Germany painted a haunting picture of things with their accounts of the fighting in Russia. Soldiers were returning to Germany on a weekly basis. Many of these men were psychologically broken and permanently damaged by their experiences. It was clear that all was not going as well as the Nazi propaganda machine would have its people believe. The situation at this point was not desperate, but it was becoming obvious to even the most patriotic of National Socialist society that things were not going as planned.

As more men enlisted for fighting their former occupations in the war industry, agriculture, government administration and civil defence had to be filled. The obvious solution to solving this problem was to mobilise Germany's women on the home front. Many young German women volunteered for various duties, carrying them out in addition to their normal employment and their obligations as mothers and housewives. Helena Koerg recalls:

> I was working more hours at the bakery as we agreed to produce extra bread which could then be shipped out to augment the food supplies of our forces in the east. As bombing raids on our cities became more frequent we were

also asked to produce more bread for soup kitchens so that they could help feed those who had been made homeless in the bombing raids. I would be working now from early morning; sometimes 4am. I would then go home briefly to make sure the girls were ready for school and Reinhard ready for his day at the pharmacy. Then, once that was done, I would return to work and be there until I had to meet the girls from school. After that I would go home with the girls, prepare a meal, then go out to my voluntary job at the hospital, where I helped care for our wounded soldiers. There were so many coming back that extra people were needed to undergo basic care training. Some of the soldiers just needed someone to be there and talk with them, and reassure them they would be okay. Many of the ones I dealt with were amputees. Some had both legs missing, others arms and legs missing. As they lay in their beds recuperating from these horrific and debilitating wounds, Iron Crosses were pinned to their pyjama tops. These men were regarded as heroes by us all, but they were broken heroes.

Gertrud came home after her Wednesday evening Hitler Youth meeting and said, "Mother, you don't have to come to the school as I will make sure my sisters get home safely. I know what I have to do in case of air or gas attack so we will be fine; you don't have to worry yourself." The Jungmadelbund had been instrumental in instructing the girls of Germany as to their duties; that they too had a role to play in their nation's survival. I reluctantly agreed that Gertrud would be responsible for bringing her younger sisters home and also doing more in the home such as helping to cook the evening meal and clearing up afterwards. As it happened this arrangement worked very well for us and I was feeling less tired and depressed by it all after a few weeks. I did feel that we could not keep this up for long. I was not getting home some nights until 10pm. I would walk home with a group of local women, with an escort to ensure we arrived home safely. Gertrud had cooked our meal and left some for me. Reinhard would make sure the girls had cleared up and then gone to bed at a sensible hour. It was a lot for them to be burdened with at such a young age. When I arrived home everyone was asleep in their beds. I sat down at the kitchen table with the plate of food Gertrud had left for me. I sat and looked at it and thought how beautiful a cook she was. I then started crying. We should not have to be doing this. As I ate and wept I thought of dear Peter again. I cried for a good thirty minutes as I ate the food. Afterwards, I washed and went to bed with a headache and feeling totally miserable.

Gertrud Koerg vividly remembers the beginnings of what were to be some extremely tough times:

I knew mother was very tired by all the things she was doing and that she could not do all of this by herself. The Jungmadelbund were saying, "Girls, you have a duty and a part to play too. You can cook and care for your younger siblings while your parents commit extra labours towards winning this war." Of course, child and home care was a major component of what we were learning at the time. We were ready for the challenges and we accepted them as a duty to the Führer and our nation. The girls of the BDM, our senior girls' movement, were doing things like helping to care for children, collecting children from school, helping people who had been bombed out of their homes, visiting soldiers in hospital and lots of other tasks. We were told that if we all pull together we will win the war but a nation has to work together and make sacrifices. I did as much as I could to help mother and take some of the pressure off her. My younger sisters were very well behaved in all. If they did play up I would raise my voice and say, "Come on now, no nonsense. Mother and father will be very angry with you." That often did the trick.

Helena Koerg was so proud of her eldest daughter but was worried by the events taking place in Germany at the time:

I thought of my Gertrud as a little girl soldier. Not only was she such a beautiful young girl, she shouldered so many adult responsibilities. I used to watch her with her young sisters and see how well she cared for them. She was amazing for a girl of such a young age. She even helped our neighbour with her newborn baby. There were days when the baby cried incessantly from morning to night. Gertrud would go round to see if she needed help and the woman was too proud to admit that she needed any. Yet Gertrud would say, "Here, I will help. Give the baby to me." Within a few minutes the baby would stop crying and would be happily gurgling in my daughter's arms. Gertrud would help the neighbour on many occasions with her new baby and her other three children. They all loved Gertrud so much. I used to sit and look at my Gertrud and think how proud of her I was.

Christmas of 1942 in Germany had not been interrupted by the war. Children still went out to sing carols, housewives still made sweetmeats and the men still drank beer. For many Germans on the home front Christmas 1942 would be their last. Many were rightly apprehensive of what the new year would bring. They year 1943 would prove a disastrous one for the German military; it would herald the slow strangulation of Hitler's Third Reich. Adeline Seidel recalled Christmas 1942 in the Kreuzberg district of Berlin:

> We never had much anyway. Our parents couldn't afford presents though the local authority would see that we did receive some treats. We were hardened to the realities of being poor. I do remember the local Nazi authorities bringing Christmas trees around for all the families who didn't have one. It was a charming gesture. They also handed out gingerbread and some extra food which had been donated by local businesses. So we did not do too badly really. We didn't want help or charity but sometimes people had to bury their pride and accept what was being offered to them. In that respect my family was no different. We didn't think we were in any real danger at that time in 1942, but 1943 was a completely different year for us. The United States had bombers based in England in preparation for operations

against German cities. It was a relatively quiet build-up of resources but we knew our enemy was gaining strength and preparing to attack from the air. Masses of heavy bombers would soon arrive to rain death and destruction from thousands of feet above. It was a year where our armies faced defeat in Russia and where I myself would become an orphan of war.

Gertrud Koerg recalls Christmas 1942, particularly the new dresses her father bought for her and her sisters and their mother Helena:

That Christmas morning we were anxious to see what presents we had. We did not expect too much as we were a country at war and understood that luxuries that would normally be given as gifts were needed elsewhere. Besides, our war production was geared completely to military supplies with little concern for anything else. I recall tearing open my present to reveal one of those dreadful Adefa Nazi-brand girl's dresses. Adefa had been an attempt at the Aryanization of the German women's fashion industry. My dress was clearly a second-hand one and its style was less than elegant in my eyes. I didn't like it at all but had to appear thrilled with the garment to prevent offending father who had bought it. My mother also had one of those dresses. In the past she had always worn dresses which had been popular with women in Paris and England. Mother later remarked to me in private, "For heaven's sake, just pretend to like it. I will have to do the same. We can't upset your father; he thinks he is doing the right thing." We agreed between us that the Adefa dresses made us look like old grannies. We laughed about them but it was not much fun having to wear them. The footwear suffered the same way as the clothing fashion. They brought out these horrible looking brown or black shoes of the type an old lady might wear. They were very uniform and lacked elegance in every respect. We had other things to worry about than those dreadful Adefa dresses and the shoes though.

Because Hitler was a committed vegetarian [...] he felt his people should follow his example and eat only meals consisting of vegetables. Vegetables were always in good supply as they could be grown anywhere. People began growing any vegetables they could around the seasons. Meat would become a little harder to acquire as the war went on. We still ate meat but everyone was talking about how we should all follow the Führer's example and eat only vegetables. This vegetable diet thing was often jokingly referred to as 'The Führer Diet'. I remember my grandfather saying how he would never give up eating his German sausage and other meats for anyone, the Führer included. With hindsight we were all being prepared for the privations to come. In a way I think the Nazi authorities were trying to prepare the German nation for the total war which they knew was coming.

Helena Koerg recalls the brief flirtation with vegetarianism:

The Führer Diet, as some of us called it, seemed a good idea at the time [...] Yet when you cooked up a meal consisting purely of this vegetable slop the men's faces would drop to their feet. They would sit there grudgingly eating it, saying how nice it was. Afterwards they would still be hungry. Men can't function without eating a proper meal. After a while even the most dedicated Nazis began to crave their meat and started eating it again. Men are strangely contradictory beasts and any housewife will understand what I mean by that. For Christmas dinner 1943 we ate roast pork. We ate very well in all with cakes to follow, which were all homemade of course. We sat at the table and prayed that the war would end before the next Christmas day arrived. The reality was that a very difficult year was looming for us in Germany. There was just this feeling.

As New Year 1943 arrived I felt a shudder through my whole body. It felt like someone had just walked over my grave. I lay in bed next to Reinhard yet couldn't sleep or settle. I began to irritate him with my restless state and he began to grumble and curse me. After an hour I got up and went downstairs. I sat in the chair watching the last embers of the fire, deep in my own thoughts. When I fell asleep I dreamt of fire, pain and suffering. I awoke in the early hours with tears running down my face. I felt scared about the future but went back upstairs to bed. I climb into bed with my back to Reinhard who immediately snuggled up against me. I felt him caressing my breasts and soon I felt an erection sticking into my back. I didn't feel like making love but I positioned myself so he could penetrate me from behind. I stimulated him by gripping the shaft of his penis with my fingers as he thrust in and out. A loud moan accompanied by the feeling of a jet of semen against my cervix heralded completion. As Reinhard drifted back to sleep, happily satisfied, I lay awake and, amongst other thoughts, hoped he had not just made me pregnant. Another child now would not be the best of things. As I lay in the comfort of the marital bed I still could not […] dispel that haunting picture I had witnessed in that earlier dream.

Chapter 7

City of Ghosts

'Watching the skies, waiting for the end.'

The sense of a coming storm in 1943 was one many Germans at home felt privately. With the steady mobilisation of the German home front many young girls and women were now enlisted into the aircraft, tank and munitions industries in their respective towns and cities. As previously mentioned, those women with children and husbands still at home had the difficult task of juggling their home lives with their obligations towards the German war effort. But if things were difficult now they would soon become a whole lot worse.

On 18 February 1943 the first public admission was made that Germany might lose the war. This came not via Allied propaganda but from the mouth of Nazi Propaganda Minister, Joseph Goebbels. Goebbels' infamous 'Total War' speech read as if it had come straight from the script of the Third Reich's own apocalyptic demise. The speech called upon the German people to fight for their very survival. It stated that the fate of the German people lay in their will to fight on, regardless of the hardships, and that the survival of a non-Jewish, non-Bolshevist Europe depended upon every man, woman and child in the Reich. It was not so much a speech as a desperate call to arms, preparing a nation to sacrifice itself. However, Goebbels' 'Total War' speech is today regarded by many Third Reich historians as one of his most powerful pieces of political rhetoric.

Helena Koerg felt grateful that she had her husband with her working on the home front, but all this was to change when, in July 1943, Reinhard Koerg received notification from the authorities that he was required to report for military training. His role as a pharmacist would be filled by one of the young women in Kassel. Helena recalls:

> This came as a terrible shock to me. I had to sit down and try and take it all in. I didn't want my man to go and fight.

I was terrified of what might happen if he didn't come home [...]. I was terrified of how the girls would react and how it might affect them. Reinhard had been called to report to the local barracks where he would begin his military training. He would remain with us until his training was complete, whereby he would then be sent to the battlefront. It was not difficult to guess where he would be sent. Our forces had been engaged in a major action against the Soviets at Kursk throughout July and August of 1943. The battle had proved somewhat inconclusive to both sides and we had lost many men and many tanks in the fighting. In a way after Kursk our armed forces were no longer capable of mounting a major offensive in the east. We did not lose the war because of Kursk but it was a contributory factor, among many others. I had to break the news to the girls about their father and they did not take it very well. Gertrud, as ever, tried to be strong for her younger sisters, but the strain upon her was immense with everything else going on at the time.

Gertrud, now aged fourteen, had joined the *Bund Deutscher Madel* (League of German Maidens), or BDM as it was known for short. She recalls:

Upon reaching the age of fourteen I joined the BDM, which was the senior sister organization to the *Jungmadelbund*. Due to the bombing raids on Kassel, which had steadily increased from 1942, we were drilled in what to do when the bombers came, and where all the main air raid shelters were located in the city. [...] after a raid we were required to go and help the wounded and those whose homes had been hit by bombs. We were taught basic first aid so we could clean and dress wounds and construct splints for suspected broken limbs and things. When my family was told our father would have to go out and fight we were devastated. We felt that his occupation may have spared him the dreaded call-up for army service but it made no difference. He was told he was going to be replaced by a young woman so he could join the war against the enemy. They didn't tell him

Adolf Hitler, the Satanic Messiah.

The fatal allure: a woman holds her daughter up to greet the Führer, 1934.

Girls of the BDM give the Führer a rapturous welcome.

Above: German troops pictured here during the invasion of Poland, September 1939.

Right: Gertrud Koerg, aged ten, poses in her *Jungmadelbund* uniform, 1939.

Above: Ilse Koerg, pictured here with her grandmother.

Left: Helga Koerg, photographed outside the Koerg's home at Kassel.

Right: A German mother
wearing her newly awarded
'Mother's Cross'.

Below: A Christmas scene in 1939.
The Führer's portrait and swastika's
form the centrepiece.

Left: Adaline Seidel as a ten-year-old member of the *Jungmadelbund*.

Below: Interference in tactical matters by Hermann Göering cost the *Luftwaffe* a victory during the Battle of Britain in 1940.

Above: Ursula Bomme, pictured third from the right.

Right: Danni Foestahl (left) relaxes with a friend.

Hilde Hermann in the BDM. She later witnessed human brains in glass jars.

ADEFA: Nazi fashion.

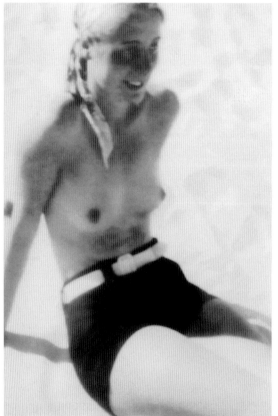

Above: A bombed street in a German city. From 1943 things would become much worse.

Left: Alessa Goberg: 'Being topless to us girls was as natural as a soldier wearing uniform.' Alessa is aged twenty-one in this photograph.

Above: As Allied air attacks on Germany increased, German women entered the German fire defence force to assist in firefighting duties.

Right: Diana Richter is pictured on the right wearing a bikini. Bernadette Junghman is on the left in photo, wearing her boyfriend's cap.

Hilde Eissner takes aim with a rifle: 'The social fabric of our society began to collapse by 1944.'

Elizabeth Schwin.

Maria Goetze at the front, holding out her hand. She survived the Battle for the Seelow Heights.

Left: The death of Nazi Germany was not a pretty sight to behold. Here, a German family hold aloft a white flag of surrender.

Below: A crowd of Germans stand in stunned silence as the occupation of their country begins, 1945.

Above: Helena Koerg, pictured post-war during a day out with her daughters: 'Mum was not happy, she was sad most of the time after the war.'

Right: Gertrud Koerg pictured post-war. Her mother, Helena, always called her 'my beautiful angel, my rock'.

Left: A post-war photograph of
Helga Koerg, taken in the 1960s.

Below: Kitka Obermann, aged
seventeen, srikes a pose in
happier times.

where he would be going but it was pretty obvious wasn't it. Also my mother made the decision to leave her bakery job. It was not easy, but the little shop was in danger of being hit by bombs. On several occasions it was nearly hit. Herr Fauschner decided to close the shop down until the war had ended. He told my mother in a mournful tone that he did not wish to be responsible for any deaths and so would close until all of this was over.

Mother went to work at the Henschel plant in the city. This company was responsible for the construction of heavy Panzer [tank] vehicles. Her going to work there worried me even more as this was a prime target for the enemy bombers. I said to my mother, "Dear mother, you do not have to do this. There has to be something else." Her eyes were always bloodshot and tired and she would just say, "Gertrud, my beautiful angel, we have no choice as we are women and we have to keep this nation of ours together. All the men are needed now and we have to take over their work." It was a sobering statement for a fourteen-year-old. My schooling became so disrupted by the threat of air attacks that soon even school stopped. I would stay home and look after my two young sisters. When the air raid warning was given I would take them to the shelter for safety and would stay with them like a mother until it was all over. The sound of the bombers coming and the flak firing scared my sisters; then the bombs began to fall [she makes a whistling noise]. My sisters would cling to me for their lives, trying to hide their heads in my jacket. Every time the ground and walls shook under the bombs I would try and reassure them, saying "it will be alright we are safe here".

Helena Koerg recalls her work at the Henschel plant in Kassel:

It was a pretty big plant and I had never been inside a factory before in my life. I was not alone as many of my female friends were working there too. You would just report for work with your papers and they would take you to where you would be working. They put me on a kind of drill which made threads in these large, heavy, square sections of metal. A stream of white industrial oil constantly ran as the drill made the threads. I would pull the handle down, make the thread, then move the one I had just done along and line another one up, and so on. It was monotonous and repetitive work and the plant I was in used to get very hot. I would tie my hair up every morning before going as one of the men there who was training us told me one girl had her scalp torn from her head when her hair became entangled in the moving machinery.

Gertrud was home most of the time as it was unsafe to be in school. Some volunteers began to teach children in the small hall at the bottom of our road. It was relatively safe there. There was a radio on. In the event of an enemy attack coming it would warn everyone. Once the warning came: "Enemy bombers approaching Kassel, twenty minutes. Repeat, twenty minutes!" The small group of children and adults had enough time to get to the main shelter and safety. At the Henschel plant we worked all day and into the evening. Some of the women would end up fainting through exhaustion and/or lack of food. You had to eat plenty or your body would just give up after time. Often we had bread, sausage, vegetables; anything really. There were always plenty of cooked potatoes, which we ate with a little salt. It was dull but it filled your stomach. As we worked, water was brought round to us at our machines. The water was often lukewarm and tainted with oil but you either drank it or went without. Anything was better than nothing to moisten your mouth and lips. We had short breaks to rest and eat.

The day was often interrupted by the air raid warning. The air raids actually became something we stupidly looked forward to. When we went down into the shelter we would sit with our heads on our arms and would go to sleep almost straight away. Often, I would be woken up by one of my friends after a raid, having not heard a thing, I would often sleep through all the noise going on outside [she laughs]. The only fear I had was for the girls back home. I knew Gertrud would be okay as she was bright and intelligent beyond her young years. Every morning I left the house I hated it though. I just wanted a normal existence again, as did many of us women. We were patriotic, of course, in support of our country and doing what we could, but how much longer could we keep going?

Ursula Bomme recalls:

In 1943 I was a twenty-year-old. All the fuss about "Why are you not married yet, Frau Bomme?" seemed to disappear under the bombing. We young women enrolled into the fire defence service. We were expected to do whatever duties we could to help our country, particularly after the bombers had been. We were given helmets and overalls and told to put them on and then they'd give you a bucket. After a raid we would assist the fire services in tackling the fires started by the bombs. Buckets of water and sand were used and we worked in teams helping to put blazing homes out. The local BDM girls would assist with the wounded or people made homeless.

I recall one raid had started some fires, which we were able to put out alongside the fire services. It was at night, and just as we had finished there were shouts of another raid almost upon us. We had not got far when bombs began to fall. The flak were already firing away and splinters of shrapnel from the exploding shells were falling to earth all around us. You had to keep your protective steel helmet on at all times. I was running with twelve other girls and one of them had her helmet in her hand and not on her head. We had not run even fifty metres when I saw her fall to the ground out of the corner of my eye. She almost cartwheeled as she fell, and I stopped, and me and four others went to her aid. A piece of flak had fallen onto her head, and because she had not been wearing her helmet it split her head open. It was a ghastly wound which was bleeding heavily. As bombs whistled down and flak guns fired I told one of the girls to shine a torch onto the wound as I tried to dress it. Then we dragged her to the nearest air raid shelter. It was a wound that she should have survived with nothing more than a headache and bruise but by the time we got her into the shelter she was dead. The girl was just nineteen years old and the shrapnel that had killed her had gone through the top of her skull and pierced the brain. There had been massive bleeding around her brain, which we could not have stopped.

I often witnessed whole 8.8-cm explosive shells falling back to earth. Many often fell harmlessly into the nearby river, while others exploded in the streets. These were faulty rounds as they were designed to detonate high in the air even if they hit nothing. We women who assisted our firefighting services were in many ways in as much danger as frontline soldiers. As more and more houses became wrecked we had to leave our homes and seek safety outside of the city where it was a little safer. It was either that or go and stay with relatives or friends.

The girls and young women who were employed in agricultural work away from the urban areas fared slightly better than their city counterparts. Alessa Goberg was a beautiful young German woman who had been brought up in an agricultural background. Four generations of her family had been hard-working farming people. Alessa had worked on the family farm ever since she could walk. She recalls:

As farming people, from young children we learned all about the land around us and it was expected of us. As a young child I learned how to milk goats and cows and look after chickens and things. When the war broke out our lives continued much as normal for the first three years or so. From 1941 we would have girls visit us to complete their Landjahr and we also had girls from the League of German Maidens here with us on rotation. It would be my job to teach them things. I was just nineteen when we had the first girls here with us. Many were excited by the prospect of being in the countryside with all the animals. Some missed their homes, of course, but I felt I was very good with them. I would do all I could to make them feel happy while they were with us, despite the hard work [...].

In the summer the day started early; often as soon as it got light. My father, Ernst, and the labourers would be up and working from first light. I would go and wake the girls up around 6.30-7am. I would make sure they were washed and had their breakfast and ready for work. They had a leader appointed to them and I often liaised with her to ensure all was running correctly. In the summer the girls learned how to harvest the crops as this was the hardest job. We grew cereal crops; wheat for bread flour, and animal feeds too. What we produced went to the markets and shops in the local towns and villages where we lived, just outside of the city of Heidelberg.

I recall in 1943 many of our able-bodied young labourers being called up for military service. I felt sad at them having to leave us, but it was for the good of the Reich. We said our farewells and hoped they would return to us the following summer. They promised to write, and many of them did. It was always exciting to receive their letters. One young man named Theodore won an Iron Cross Second Class within a week of joining battle. To replace the male labourers we had more girls and women. Some of them had never even seen a cow in real life before and they were afraid of them. Some didn't want to get their hands dirty at all. I used to make them squirm in horror when I would pick up horse shit from our yard with my bare hands. I would tell them, "Look, it's nothing. It's just chewed grass really." We would also slaughter our own livestock and they did not like this much either. To us it was just another job one had to learn as part of our way of life. Of course the girls loved the meat that we spared for their meals later on.

In all, the many women who came to help us work the farm worked very hard indeed. On a Saturday afternoon we would try and get everything done early so we could go into Heidelberg town for some rest and fun. Sunday was another working day as we still had animals to feed and water, but late afternoon we had time to ourselves. Some of the women went to church, others sat and made corn dolls or wrote letters home. We had a lake on our property which we could swim in. The water was refreshing on hot days and we often swam with no clothes on as there were no men around [she laughs]. Afterwards we would often sit and sunbathe without our tops on. It was perfectly natural for us to do this. The city girls found this difficult as they lived in different ways to us, but many of them soon found it a delight to sunbathe topless.

In late 1943 there was a definite change in our lives due to the war going on. We had been largely untouched until the US Air Force attacks gained momentum. The bombers would often jettison bombs over farmland, ignorant of the fact people lived there too. Many of the bombs exploded in the fields, but they killed cattle and other animals which were highly valuable to us. My father was furious when one of his prize stud cattle was killed by bombs which had been jettisoned by a US plane. He phoned the authorities and complained about this. A few days later several flak guns arrived and took up positions in the fields a mile or so away from our buildings and home. I took some of the girls down the fields with me to see them and take them some bread and milk. The flak gunners were very young men indeed and they took quite a shine to us. Their presence only became a concern when one warm day, after we had been swimming in the lake, I was sitting topless when I noticed one of them watching us through his binoculars. I jumped to my feet and ran after him shouting at him, "Hey you, dirty little devil. Come here." We watched him scurrying away on his hands and knees, through a hedge he thought he could hide in and not be seen [she laughs].

The next time we went to visit the gunners there was quite an awkward silence. I asked which one of them had been looking at us. The boy's friends all pointed to the one boy, laughing, and said, "It was him, not us." I walked up to the red-faced young man and said to him, "Maybe next time you should join us." There was more laughter and this poor young man had nowhere to hide. He was actually very nice and introduced himself as Walter Eickhert. He was twenty years of age. When we left we could hear Walters's friends still tormenting him. It made me smile as we rode our bicycles back down the narrow lane. I knew a few girls who would sneak down the fields to spend time with the flak boys. I never told on them as I did it myself [she laughs]. Everyone asked what we got up to. We often tried their uniform jackets on and things. Sometimes they would take photographs of us for their families back home. I became intimate with Walter Eickhert on a few occasions. Most of the time I let him kiss me on the lips. He always wanted more but I knew I had to be very careful as my parents followed a strict Catholic religious theory. If they had ever known I had been down the fields kissing a young man there is every possibility they would have sent me to a convent for punishment. That did happen back then a lot. I gave the young man hand relief on several occasions and he was more than happy with that. In fact I became quite skilled at hand relief over the months [she laughs].

However, there was little time for romance as more food was required to feed Germans at this time and we were working longer hours. To make things worse the American bombers were now being escorted by single-seat fighter aircraft. They used to have fun with our farms, usually on the return trip from bombing Heidelberg. Some of the fighter planes would sweep across the tree tops at very low level and fire their machine guns into our buildings and grain stores. They also shot cattle and any other livestock that happened to be there. This I understood, in a way, as these were our resources and their job was to cut those resources off to make life difficult for us. Killing the animals though was something I can never forgive. We would have to collect up the carcasses of the dead animals and use what we could as we could not waste anything. We were warned to be vigilant about Allied fighter bomber aircraft. There had been many incidents of horses and carts being blown up along roads. I was told, "Those Americans won't care what you are doing if you are carrying grain to market or some food stuffs to a local hospital or something. They will shoot you up without any hesitation. Do not try and travel in horse-drawn carts in the daylight hours for your own safety." All the women were briefed as to the dangers we now faced, but we had to continue working in the fields and work out how we could still work and be safe from attack from the air.

The flak gunners had claimed a few enemy aircraft that had been harassing us over the weeks. One young American pilot was captured alive. One of our women wanted to shoot him for his 'criminal acts', as she called them. We were all very angry and wanted to beat this man, but when we first set eyes on him as he was brought up to the house we just felt pity for him. He looked terrified and thought we would kill him. Instead he was given a drink and checked for any injuries. Apart from some cuts and bruises from landing in trees in his parachute he was fine. We just stood and stared as some of our soldiers arrived to take the young American away for questioning. His war was over now and he would be sent on to a prisoner-of-war camp somewhere. After that we did not see too many fighter bombers over our area.

The winter was very tough for us that year, but we did what work we could do. Sometimes we were short of labour as many girls fell ill with colds and flu and couldn't work. All the time we had more coming in, but at times there was too little to do. When the days are short and weather bad all you can do is tend the animals as best as you can, plant what crops you can and keep going forward, hoping this wretched war will soon end. Hitler was insisting his farmers focus on the production of vegetables over meat. Being a vegetarian, he felt all Germans should follow his way with their diet. The problem was Germans love their meat and few could ever have given it up, even for their Führer. Meat did become somewhat scarce later on and even potatoes became like gold. Later on we had to guard the potato crops from thieves who would then sell them on the very lucrative black market in the towns and cities. Those of us who could shoot were given guns and, along with my father, we patrolled the crop fields. We often saw the evidence of where thieves had been taking our crops, or rather the people's crops. They were hard to catch in the act, even at night. If they heard us coming they would be gone before we could even see them. Sometimes we would be up all night doing this and then working in the daytime. We had to keep trying to produce for the growing needs of the German home front. Our nation's survival depended heavily upon our work, though most of what we grew went to the military first. The soldiers were considered the most in need of food and the ordinary people secondary. The ordinary people at home in the towns, cities and villages were all encouraged to grow their own vegetables as much as possible and to make sacrifices. Without the women I worked with the food would have become much scarcer [...].

Another young woman. Petra Oerbergh. aged nineteen and from Berlin, recalls how, by 1943, life revolved around the steadily increasing bombing of the city:

The bombing severely limited what activities you could do. Many of the schools were closed as it was just too dangerous for children to attend school by this point. The Hitler Youth had begun to set up special camps outside the city in countryside areas. Many children were then evacuated to these camps. They were still subject to Hitler Youth authority and carried out their same Hitler Youth duties. Many of their parents remained in and around the city, working in the war effort or assisting with home front tasks under the direction of the local authorities. No one could get away from doing their duty. I remember my parents did not want to leave their home. They moved all essential items down into the cellar. That is where we went when an air raid alert was given.

Many have asked, "What was it like?" I can still vividly remember how, if you had a radio set – which my father did – they would tell you exactly where the bombers were and how many minutes until they were over us. They would even tell you how big the raid was going to be. The first signs of trouble coming were the sounds of the flak guns firing at the bombers. There was a very heavy concentrated belt of flak artillery around Berlin. Guns of all sizes were in place to engage high-, medium- and low-flying targets.

I popped my head outside just once and heard the bombers coming. It was like a rumbling sound, a drone that oscillated in its tone. As I continued looking up into the blue sky all these white contrails came into view. It was a magnificent sight; if it were not so deadly. You could clearly see the black spots of exploding flak shells amongst these contrails. Then the nightmare began; the first bombs whistling down earthward. I jumped back down into the cellar and slammed the entrance door shut behind me. In the dim light of a small lamp the steadily increasing sound of exploding bombs could be heard. They got closer and closer and the noise louder and louder. I was on my own on this occasion and there was a tremendous explosion which shook the small lamp from my hands. It smashed on the floor of the cellar and luckily for me it fell onto bare stone floor. It had little fuel inside it and this soon burned out and it was now pitch black. I could taste dust on my lips and I wiped it away but the smell of smoke was coming through too. I sat beneath our home in that cellar for almost two hours, too afraid to move, the ground shaking like an earthquake might. When I tried to open the door to the cellar I could not move it. I began to panic in the darkness and began to shout "help, help". But no one answered. It was lucky my father had brought matches and candles and some supplies down there. Feeling around in the darkness with my hands, I was able to locate matches and a candle and light the candle so that I could see. There was a little food but I did not want to touch this unless I really had to. I had lost all sense of time but tried to work out by how long the candle had been burning.

I was trapped down in that cellar for three days. I knew I couldn't lift the door and guessed something had happened up above. I knew my parents would come so I was not too worried. On the third day I heard faint voices up above and then scratching sounds. I heard the familiar voices of mother and father. Mother was crying and shouting, "Quickly! Get that off there, please. Please be quick." I began shouting, "I'm down here! Please open this damn door and get me out of here." After another agonising wait I could hear someone pulling the cellar door and then a chink of light shining through. As the door was pulled open by the rescue services all I could see was daylight shining through. The rest of our home had been destroyed by a bomb. My father grabbed my hand and pulled me out of the cellar. He began to cry quite hysterically, asking me if I was hurt or anything. I told him I was fine and then mother was holding onto me and crying. It was an emotional time.

Many families had not been so lucky. As we walked away from the rubble of our home, through thick, grey smoke that hung like a blanket, we saw the corpses of whole families being pulled out of the rubble. We tried to help pull bricks and other pieces out of the way along with other people. All we found beneath all of the debris were corpses. Little children still clinging to their mothers. Most of the dead had no visible signs of injury. One little girl had blood running from out of her ears and her mouth. I will never, ever forget her face as her lifeless body was pulled from her dead mother's arms. Rigor mortis had begun to set in and it took three men to separate the child's corpse from the arms of her mother who had been trying to protect her. An amputated leg still complete with a shoe on its foot was also pulled from the rubble. That scene was my recurring nightmare from then onwards.

With our home destroyed we were invited to live with friends. We accepted their offer but we knew all too well that those corpses we had seen and helped pull out of their wrecked home could be us next time. Some women had already set up a kind of soup kitchen and were cooking soup and preparing potatoes and bread for the community. In all this devastation there were women trying to help, to try and make people's lives bearable and send a message that we would not be beaten into submission. I helped wherever I could, and I volunteered as a driver to take wounded people to hospitals and move families out of the city. If you could drive they would get you to do all these things. The back of the vehicle was also used to transport dead bodies away from the scene. There was a danger of disease breaking out so bodies were removed and buried, usually in a large, mass grave in the city. There was no time for ceremony. Now we knew we had to be hard and resilient and take this as it came. Victory, they would say, would be born through our suffering.

As we worked, clearing up the debris of war and helping injured people and families, we often cursed those in charge. One young woman once said to me, "Petra, please tell me who are suffering the most, us or them?" So I asked her, "Who do you mean by them?" She just had that look of anger in her eyes and replied rather sarcastically, "Hitler and his fucking gang." I told her, "Be quiet. If someone hears you say that you will be joining those people in one of the camps. They are not holiday camps, you know. They are killing people in some of those places." She asked me how I knew that so we both went and got ourselves a hot, black coffee and found a quiet spot where we could talk. I explained to her that the Sachsenhausen facility outside Berlin was a good example of why one should ask no questions or talk in a bad away of the Führer or any of those in his government. She then retorted, "But this explains little, Petra". So I said to her, "That smell that you can detect coming from that place; what do you think it is? It is the perfume of corpses, a scent which we shall soon have to wear and a scent which we too could become unless we keep our mouths shut, keep our ideas to ourselves and just get on with what we are doing." I remember her reaction afterwards. She took a swig of coffee, pulled this funny face, and said, "This tastes like fucking piss and I care not about Jews or anyone else or this fucking war."

Adeline Seidel and her family had a near miss with death during an air attack on Berlin in late 1943:

Things had not been good in the past but now we were involved in a major war we had the constant threat from the bombers. My parents went to work in the nearby factories, despite all the dangers they faced each day by doing so. The warning system we had was very good and gave you adequate time to evacuate your home or workplace. On one particular raid I decided I was going to remain in our home in a cupboard beneath the stairs. This was something even the English families would do. So when we received warning of a large incoming force of heavy bombers I went into the cupboard. As I sat in the darkness a voice just kept saying, "Get out of here. Go to the big shelter used by the staff at the factory." I was meant to be at my grandparents because my parents were at the factory, but had decided to come home early. I sat in the dark cupboard battling with my thoughts, then I just got up and burst out of the cupboard, out of the back yard and down the road. The guns were already firing in the distance so I knew I had little time. When I arrived at the shelter there was a man outside just about to slam the door shut. He spotted me running down the road and shouted, "Get in here, you stupid little girl! Did you not hear the warnings?" I ran inside and the heavy door slammed shut and I ran on down the flights of steps into the belly of the shelter. Down there were many friends, and after a few minutes I found my mother. Her face was black and oily from her work on the machines. We hugged and she kissed me and we sat down and just waited. It was late afternoon and I was tired and drifted off to sleep in my mother's arms. I was woken some twenty minutes or so later by a terrible series of explosions. These just seemed to go on and on. The lights went off and on but there was a generator, so as long as that was okay we would have light down here. It was a yellowy, nicotine-coloured light that made everyone's faces inside appear jaundiced. Old men, old women, women with babies and children just sat staring up at the ceiling as the bombs rained down. I remember an old couple huddled in a corner. The old man held the old woman's hands, offering some reassurance that all would be okay. They looked so dejected; in fact we all must have looked that way.

When it was all over we came out into a scene from hell itself. All that remained was just fire and rubble. Our home was gone and broken sewers ejected their filth into the streets. People wandered around dazed, and confused about what to do or where to go. They covered their faces with anything they had as the smell was appalling. Some girls from the Bund Deutscher Madel came and gave us hot drinks and blankets. One told me, "You are not safe here; you must come with us. There are camps outside the city where you can be looked after and where you will be safer. Your mother and father will know where you are. They need to stay here for their work duties but you can come with us." I looked at my parents and both of them said, almost at the same time, "Take her with you. She will be safer out of the city and away from the bombs." My parents had to write my details down and sign a document for me. The BDM girl then held my hand and smiled at me and told me, "Everything will be alright but we have to go." I then I walked away from my parents with the girls I would come to call "my sisters".

That was the last time I would see my dear mother and father. […] I kept looking back at them until they became obscured by the smoke from burning buildings and I could see them no more. They became like ghosts and I felt as if I had already become an orphan. I felt like crying all the time. The BDM girls sensed my sadness and kept talking to me. God bless them, they were so nice and they looked after me as if I was their own flesh and blood. That is why I can only ever refer to them as sisters. At the camp, which was situated on farmland, the BDM girls ate with me and slept beside me, and constantly looked after me to make sure I was alright. At that point in my life I don't think I could have carried on without them. I can say that, looking back on things, I had left what was becoming a city, not of people but ghosts.

Chapter 8

Sumpfwascher!

As with all communities caught up in the tragedy of war, many German towns, cities and villages would become largely devoid of males but Hitler's housewives did their utmost to help support their own families and communities as well as the country's war effort. Many German women who had husbands or boyfriends fighting in the war were naturally very patriotic and did all they could to support their armed forces. As previously mentioned, they formed help groups and volunteered to take on extra jobs in the factories or labouring on farms. Any job a man could do German women were soon doing on the home front. Released from the shackles of the old Nazi motto of children, church and the kitchen, many German women proved vital in solving the various challenges encountered both on the home front and on the battlefront. Yet there were always those who were classed as outcasts in society. Diana Richter recalls:

> I had been doing secretarial jobs throughout my late teens.
> I had never imagined ever setting foot inside a large factory
> and the mere thought of it horrified me. When manpower
> became short due to the demands placed upon Germany
> by the war it was something women […] had to adapt to.
> I had a boyfriend aged twenty-three who was in the German
> Army. He had been away at the battlefront for over a year.
> That is a long time for any couple to remain apart. His
> name was Paulus Frisch and we had spoken of marriage
> before he went away. Paulus left on my twentieth birthday
> and I had hoped I would see him after a month or so, but
> a year passed and I had still not seen him. He wrote to me
> as much as he could but his letters were always somewhat
> vague in content. We lived in the city of Essen in the Ruhr,

in the west of Germany. I left my job as a typist in an office in 1944, on my father's advice. He used to say, "Young lady, you can do more useful things than write letters all day." He was referring to the nearby Krupp munitions works, which needed women to come and work on the production lines in the plant. Krupp manufactured all kinds of weapons in their factories and, convinced I was helping the war effort, I went along and spoke to the men in charge. By 1944 only the really skilled or essential German male workers remained in the factory. To plug gaps in non-skilled labour sections we women were brought in, and slave labourers were also used.

The women I encountered in the factories were a mixed group. Many were like me, just trying to do their part to support our armed forces. Others were married girls whose husbands were fighting in the war and who began sleeping with factory bosses and directors. Many of them made no secret of this and did not seem to care. In what sense they profited from giving their favours I cannot say. Most of the bosses and directors were old married men and the thought of having sex with them for extra things made me feel sick.

I recall one woman in particular who lived near us. They called her 'Blonde Rose' though I will not mention her name as she may still have relatives alive here. She had been married for a few years and had two children. I heard that her husband had divorced her on the grounds of infidelity. She was very pretty and when she was younger she used to be very thin with long, slender legs. She had long, blonde hair, which she would fashion into two plaits. Her blue eyes were also quite captivating as the black pupils seemed very large compared to most girls' eyes. It was like they were fully dilated all the time. As she grew older she battled with a weight problem and would put on weight easily. Her two daughters were a funny pair too. The youngest appeared to be in a constant state of melancholy while the older one was a totally horrible and spoiled brat, as you would say in England.

At Krupp's she turned up for work whenever she pleased, unlike the rest of us. I often saw her scurrying into private offices with men old enough to be her father. You would hear the door lock behind her and it was obvious what was going on inside the office. Me and my friends had known her for some years growing up in Essen. After her short marriage ended she gained a reputation for offering the fruit of her thighs to both males and females. She was bisexual and many girls later admitted sleeping with her after the war. One woman I know said that Blonde Rose was the best sex she ever had and better at making love than any man she had met. I recall how some young men of our community vied like stags for the attention of this woman. They brawled outside public houses where she would stand and watch the men fight until there was a clear winner. The winner would then enjoy the opportunity of walking her home and staying the night with her.

Blonde Rose was also often accused of being a marriage wrecker as she preferred the challenge of seducing married men over the single ones. Once she had got what she wanted she would appear to lose interest almost straight away. Many of the local women hated her with a passion. She earned several nicknames which included "Feel Good Fanny", "Dirty Dog", "Fuck for Free Frieda" and *Sumpfwascher*". One of the married men who had been romantically linked with her said of her, "When you looked into those huge, blue eyes it was like staring into some kind of featureless desert or a stagnant pool of water. Yet, unlike a desert, her eyes were totally devoid of warmth. Her eyes […] were merely the portals into what must have been a world of misery. She expressed little in the way of warmth or compassion toward those unlucky enough to have fallen in love with her. She treated them in a vile manner. Oh yes, she was an unpleasant woman in that respect." Another remarked, "Lying on her back after the act of sex she resembled an up-turned cart that the horse had destroyed in the process of bolting." It was said her kisses were passionate yet forceful, as if she were drawing the nutrients from the bodies of her lovers via their lips, like some form of human arachnid. When she kissed she often drew blood and to her suitors it often felt more an act of envenomation than a prelude to making love. Post coital she refused to lie in the arms of the men she had intercourse with. She would wash and dress quickly and was eager that the man leave.

I recall one incident involving Blonde Rose and a local married man. The wife discovered her husband's infidelity and shortly after found out that he had been seeing Blonde Rose. She went crazy and went off to confront Blonde Rose. There was a fight and the two women grappled. They ended up on the floor, struggling with one another and ripping chunks of each other's hair out. Blonde Rose came off worse on this occasion. Her opponent had managed to wrestle her down and was sat astride her, holding her down on the dusty ground by both wrists, screaming all kinds of obscenities in her face. Blonde Rose was clearly exhausted by this point, panting like a dog might after a hard run and unable to fight back any longer. I remember one of the women casually munching on an apple as she watched the fight.

Luckily for Blonde Rose some stranger passed by in his car and saw what was going on. He slammed on his brakes, jumped out of his car and demanded the two women stop at once. I noticed this man was wearing a leather coat and was wearing a gold Nazi Party badge on the left lapel of his coat. He must have been someone important who just happened to be passing through. Blonde Rose slowly got to her feet, brushing the dust off her dress. She had a stream of blood running from one nostril and a cut to her mouth. The two women were told, "You are a disgrace brawling in public like a pair of drunken idiots. What is this all about?" he demanded to know. The vengeance-seeking woman then pointed at Blonde Rose and said, "Ask that fat *sumpfwascher*". *Sumpfwascher* means 'bog scrubber' in English. I'm not sure where she got this slang term for a loose woman but it made me laugh as I watched with the others from the sidelines. Even the stranger had to stifle a smile at what the woman said. The only one who wasn't smiling was Blonde Rose. After the stranger had finished telling them off, Blonde Rose limped off, home holding her back and looking as if she was going to cry. When the stranger had driven off […] the other woman shouted at Blonde Rose, "If you ever mess with my man again I am going to fucking kill you."

Blonde Rose was not put off by this very public altercation. It appears that her behaviour was somewhat ignored in the toxic atmosphere of late-war Germany. Bernadette Junghmann, a close friend of Diana Richter, who also lived in Essen, recalled the woman referred to as Blonde Rose:

> I once befriended the girl. Unlike most of those in our community, I felt a little sorry for her. I felt she was like a little girl lost. I offered her friendship and support not long after she and her husband separated. I just felt sorry for her and her girls. I knew she had a reputation for being promiscuous, but that did not really bother me too much at the time. The last time I visited her was one evening in August of 1944. I went around to her house with a few things for her two girls. The girls were in bed by the time I arrived so I was not able to give them the things I had brought for them personally. Blonde Rose spoke of how her room was bleak and she wanted advice on how best to decorate it. When we entered her bedroom it possessed a kind of warm, stagnant atmosphere. It felt as if I had just entered a large reptile vivarium. Her bed was unmade, with the blue sheets all pulled to the one side […]. I offered suggestions on what she might do to improve her room but she sat beside me, just staring at me intently. Again this did not bother me at all. There was some slight concern when she left the room for a few minutes and returned wearing her dressing gown. I asked why she had changed and she told me, "Because I am feeling hot." Then she said, "All this hot weather makes me feel aroused all day long," and "there are no men around to satisfy me." She again came and sat beside me and allowed her nightgown to fall open to reveal her breasts. I asked her, "What on God's earth are you doing?" She didn't reply but proceeded to kiss me on the mouth. I know I should have pushed her away at this

point, but I didn't. Before I knew what was happening she had pushed me down onto the bed and her fingers were down between my thighs. I struggled for a minute or so then became lost in the moment. Afterwards I quickly got up and shouted at her, "You shouldn't have done that." She smiled and said, "Well, you were not complaining, were you." I left the room, slammed the door behind me and, just as I was leaving through the front door, her eldest daughter appeared. She just looked at me and asked, "Have you been with mother?" I don't know, I just leaned towards the child, kissed her on the cheek and said, "It's alright, just go back to sleep now, child."

I later heard that Blonde Rose frequently took women back to her home for sex. Not all stayed for the pleasure and had I been older and not so naïve I would not have gone to her home and allowed what happened to have happened. I thought she was a friend and I wanted to help her because so many people were so horrible to her. I was a stupid young girl aged just seventeen and felt I wanted to help, what with the war going on and things. The only person I felt I could trust to tell about this was Diana, who I regarded as my best friend. When I told Diana she wanted to go and confront Blonde Rose about it. I had to beg her not to go and cause any trouble. I told her to think of that woman's two little girls. They were the ones I really felt a terrible empathy for.

In January 1945 Blonde Rose was found dead on a deserted farm track. Her body was partially naked and most of her long, blond locks ripped out, leaving a bloodied scalp. There were no visible wounds on her body other than her scalp. The local police and Nazi authorities had far greater worries than the body of a woman generally despised and described as loose being found dead. A number of local people, both men and women, were questioned by the police but the mystery surrounding her death would never be solved. In the chaos of war nobody really cared and the cause of death was given as suicide. Diana Richter recalls: 'My mother told me local women were behind Blonde Rose's death. There were people who knew the truth, but as in many small communities they kept a vow of silence. There were no reports on her death; nothing at all. I know the girls went to live with their father after their mother's death. Maybe for them it was a blessing, a deliverance of sorts.'

Monika Graff, from Meiderich near Duisburg, recalls another woman who was branded a *sumpfwascher*, known locally as 'The Goat Lady':

> The Goat Lady used to boast of having a Romany Gypsy heritage, until the Nazis came to power when she denied all knowledge of having made such a remark. She lived alone and kept a small herd of goats. She used to make cheese from the goats' milk and sold the milk. She was not really what you would call an attractive woman but the men used to say "that woman has a great arse and tits," and that "you don't have to look into the fire when you are poking it." Many local men were seen coming and going from her house, clearly after having had sex with her. There were also rumours that she had several abortions, all carried out by herself. I am not sure how true this was, but I recall my mother telling me about it. The Goat Lady appeared to avoid the scrutiny of the local authorities. It is believed she often bribed her way out of trouble by giving local police and Nazi officials free goat's milk and cheese. My mother said that The Goat Lady did do a lot to help the local community on the home front and carried out various voluntary jobs as she was a very hard worker. My mother told me that, sometime in winter of 1944, the police arrested her. One of the officers was heard to say to her before bundling her into his car, "Fraulein, you will not be fucking your way out of this one." No one knew what happened to her but it is believed she was taken to Ravensbruck concentration camp. Maybe her past had finally caught up with her. I don't know.

Gerda Rauschilde, the twenty-three-year-old wife of a German Army Officer, also from Essen, recalled:

> Women of ill repute existed in all societies. Ours was no different other than it had strict controls placed upon it and was closely observed by the state, or rather its executors.

There were women we did not like in our communities and this was for many reasons. As a community at war there were always those who couldn't quite fit in. I recall one who had the surname Ridzich; I think her first name was Zara. I don't think she was of pure German ancestry. I am sure her mother was Croatian by birth. Her husband was German and I know he was serving in the Luftwaffe as a flak crewman. They used to live near us and the woman and her children always had a hard time with the authorities for non-compliance. We used to feel sorry for the husband. The woman's son I knew quite well as he was in the same Hitler Youth troop as my son. The leader of the troop described him as "a fat useless cry-baby". He was, in fact, rejected by the local Hitler Youth. At school they called him "fat head" as he was of below average intelligence compared to the other children and was short but large. The daughter was a horrible girl; venomous is too good a word for her. She was ill tempered, unhygienic, promiscuous, lazy and the Bund Deutscher Madel rejected her too, on the grounds she was wholly unsatisfactory and suffering from an extreme form of Oedipus complex.

None of that family, apart from the husband who was not there much, were really prepared to help on the home front in any way. They were just too concerned with themselves. The other women used to say to her, "How is your boy so fat?" The mother was always causing trouble with local men too. She would sleep with them for money or whatever else and cared not that she was sleeping with another woman's man. She had no shame and hard as we tried to warn her there would be consequences for her actions, she ignored us. When we were learning how to tackle fires caused by fire bombs she was only interested in her own world. She was able to get away with it for a while. Someone once told me that there was serious mental illness in the family bloodline. There was talk of fake birth certificates and all kinds of things. One day the three of them vanished without trace. A new family moved into the cottage where they had lived. When I asked the new family where the Ridzich family had gone they just shrugged their shoulders and replied, "We have no idea who you are talking about. We have never heard of these people." I never even saw the husband again, so what became of them I don't know. If you did not play the game as a woman back in those times it was quite easy for the authorities to make you vanish without trace. Nobody would really care if you were trouble to the neighbourhood, or lazy or promiscuous. The other women would just say, "Good riddance. She was a *sumpfwascher* that one was."

Horst Kopfel, who was involved in Luftwaffe research projects at the Rechlin facility from 1943 to 1944, recalled his visits home on leave to Magdeburg:

For a young man in a nice uniform with plenty of money in his pocket you could have the pick of any girl you wanted. This was especially true from the mid to late war years. When I went on leave I often avoided the big cities for the obvious reasons. Many were being bombed to the ground and there were little comfort to be had in such places. The smaller countryside towns were another story. I could sleep at a nice inn and the local women would be attracted to me 'like a fly to shit', as they used to say [he laughs]. I knew many of the girls who were showing an interest in me were married and had husbands who were fighting in the war. This did not always stop them from inviting me back into their homes.

I recall one terrific beauty of a girl. I could not believe my luck when she came and talked with me. It was obvious she was attracted to me so, when she asked me to go home with her, I was unable to resist. I know it was wrong but I was a young, red-blooded man back then. This girl was a tall, athletic, blonde with blue eyes and she always wore a white dress. She told me she was twenty years of age. I was twenty-four at that time. We left the inn where I had been staying and we walked, arm-in-arm, down the quiet roads to her home. Her home was well kept with a nice flower garden. There was a small air raid shelter in the back garden. No sooner had we got through the door [...] than she pounced upon me like a lion. She was muttering that it had been so long since she had been in the company of a man. I had to tell her, "Please be careful you don't damage my uniform," as I was worried she would tear the buttons and ribbons in her haste to get my clothes off. She took me by the hand and led me up the stairs and onto her bed. I was more than ready for her [he laughs] and she wasted no time in jumping on top of me and guiding me inside her. It was animal type sex and she was saying "suck my nipples," and "harder, harder" as we had sex on her bed. I spent the next few days with her and it was just sex several times a day and night. By the time I had to get my transport back to Rechlin I had a pain in my groin from all of the activity. I had never heard of the term '*sumpfwascher*' that you have mentioned. It is likely that different communities of women used different terms. That young lady was certainly no *sumpfwascher* though. I think she was just bored and missed the physical side of a relationship, which she was no longer able to have at that time.

Ursula Topf recalled how many young women were used in their communities by the local Nazi authorities:

I won't mention any names or places here, but there was a certain *burgermeister* who used his position in our town to his own advantage. The problem was he was protected by powerful people, so you could not speak out about him. If he felt you were not doing enough as a woman within the community he would summons you to report to his offices. I knew full well what that would mean. You would be blackmailed to have sexual intercourse with the man. He went through a few of the young girls in our town and one told me what happened to her after being called to his offices. She told me this:

I was fighting hard to control what was a rapidly building bottleneck of emotions. I was shown to a room, and as I entered it the heavy door slammed shut behind me and

I heard the clicking of a key being turned in the lock. At that point I knew there was no going back, no escape. I felt like some form of nocturnal insect held within the deadly embrace of a spider's web. He undressed himself, revealing a low hanging paunch which obscured his manhood. His chest was covered with a thick mat of greying hairs. I was told, "You can either comply, give me what I want and walk away, or we can address serious matters of non-compliance with state orders." I was a victim in his puppet court of blackmail. What could I do? I felt sickened at the sight of this balding, ageing man. I asked him what he wanted me to do and he asked me to follow him into another room adjacent to the one we were in. A single bed stood in a corner. He insisted I undress and go and lie down. I did as he told me. I was frightened of what would happen if I refused and caused any trouble. He had a swastika wrapped around his waist and cast it aside as he walked towards me on the bed. He clumsily mounted me, like some oversexed sea lion, and tried to have sex with me. I was too dry and he was unable to enter. He shouted, "For God's sake, do something about this." The combination of fear and anxiety made this act of what is technically rape an impossibility. He got up and left the room for a few seconds before returning, rubbing something upon his short, stubby manhood. Again he climbed upon me, his manhood short but really hard. I felt the lips part and was totally void of any sensation or any sense of pleasure. His violent thrusting then began to hurt. He complained he couldn't get in me deep enough and forced my legs further back and apart. He grunted, "You are dry, tight, and terribly uncomfortable. You have all the elasticity of a sphincter." I just wanted it to be over and I shut my eyes and tried to think of anything to take my mind off what was happening. When he was done he resembled a big panting dog. I was warned to say nothing and that everything would be alright if I kept silent. The usual story they threatened you with to shut you up.

If only Hitler knew about this. Maybe he does know about this? If there was one consolation, I learned that, after the capitulation, that old beast was found dead with four gunshot wounds to the chest. At least in some way justice had been done. It is possible one of the women he blackmailed had sought her revenge in the chaos of the last hours of the war. I didn't know and didn't care. I did tell his wife what he did though, as she trudged away from the remains of her home, clutching the few possessions she could save. I think she knew what her husband had been doing. Her opulent lifestyle could only ever have been protected by her loyalty to him. She stared coldly back at me, said nothing and carried on walking. I turned and spat on her back and said to her, "You *sumpfwascher*" and that gave me immense satisfaction.

Chapter 9

The Wolf at the Door

In many respects the wartime conditions in Nazi Germany, particularly from late 1943, provided an environment in which corruption could flourish and the unscrupulous profit. Such conditions were not unique; other countries were feeling much the same social privations brought about by the war. There were property landlords who were prepared to take all manner of bribes in lieu of payment if a woman could not afford to pay her rent. A black market in certain everyday goods and foodstuffs had begun to emerge as a result of the shortages. There were those prepared to use violence and blackmail as a means of procuring what they needed. This clinical emancipation from the constraints of the Nazi moral high ground was, sadly, a trait that would remain a scourge in Germany for many years after the Second World War had ended.

Hilde Eissner was a twenty-two-year-old mother of two from Heidelberg and recalled how, from 1944, the social fabric of Nazi Germany had begun to slowly wear away:

> Keeping the wolf from the door was an old saying that was very appropriate if you lived in Germany back in1944. If the factory, or wherever you were working, was bombed and you could not earn you were in trouble. Many of our men were fighting in the war and were away from home for the duration. In December of 1943 I had learned that my husband had been taken prisoner by the Russians. I had received the news via a simple typed letter. He was alive but there was no indication as to whether he was well or not. The only money I had left was rapidly running out. Food was becoming scarce and, as a consequence, more expensive, which in turn created a black market. The things you could buy on the black market, if you had the funds available,

were quite astounding. I once saw a case containing tinned fish, quality cigarettes, vegetables, meat and fruit. The man would show you what there was and give you his prices. Oh yes, it was all there if you had the money to buy it, but most of it was beyond my means. They would often offer you things and if you had no money they would say "well you can have this or that if I can have you".

After the last of my savings went to pay my landlord that was it. I had to take any work I could find and there was no guarantee you would even be paid afterwards. I had to send my two children to live with my parents while I struggled on. The landlord of the small block of [...] cottages preyed on the vulnerable women. You could not complain to the local Nazi Party or police as he had affiliations within these organizations. They often accepted bribes from him. You would end up in even bigger trouble if you tried to report him. He came to me one morning and I told him, "I have no money left. The father of my children is a prisoner of war. What do you expect me to be able to do about it?" He stood there in all his finery thinking for a minute. You could almost read what was on his mind. He then said, "Well, there are alternatives if you don't have the money. I am a reasonable man." I asked him what he meant by 'alternatives', to which he replied, "Oh. come on, woman, even you should know this." It then dawned on me what he meant. I felt frightened and threatened by this man. I knew in a way that, as much as I loathed this man thirty years my senior, I was stuck with either compliance or finding myself out of our home. My parents did not have much money so I could not have gone to them. Besides, they already had the children and lived too far away anyway. That man was like a fox sensing blood in a hen house. He then said, "I will leave you a day to think it through and will be back tomorrow evening." This was a real strain and trying to sleep in that empty house, thinking of my husband constantly and missing my children terribly, I felt as if I were going to fall apart.

That evening I sat out in my back garden, chain smoking cigarettes, trying to ponder my future. I was so deep in thought that I did not notice my elderly neighbour coming round to see if I was alright. I was startled when he said, "Hilde, is everything alright?" I was so upset that I just started crying. I sat there with my head in my hands, sobbing, for several minutes. My poor old neighbour did his best to console me. He then sat down and I told him everything that had been happening [...]. He was visibly shocked when I told him what the landlord had said to me and he reassured me that he could sort things out. He explained his son had connections with the local government and promised he could sort things for me and get that 'ogre', as he called him, off my back. Our conversation was momentarily interrupted by the rumble of enemy aircraft in the night sky. We were quite safe as the bombers were heading for Mannheim and Ludwigshafen. We sat and watched the searchlights as they clicked on one by one. Then the flak guns began firing at the enemy planes. My neighbour remarked, "Hmm, quite some show, isn't it, Hilde? But those poor souls in those cities will not be thinking so. Thank God there is nothing for them to bomb where we are." The bombers had appeared to split into two waves and were attacking Mannheim and Ludwigshafen at the same time. We finally went back inside our homes after watching the raid in progress for some minutes.

I was fearful of what the next day might bring and was dreading the landlord's visit. I had made the decision that if he asked me to sleep with him for payment I would have no choice but to leave and go to my parents. I was pleasantly surprised that when he returned he did so with a completely different manner. He was apologetic and remorseful over his words of the previous day. Feeling slightly relieved, I went to see my neighbour, who was smiling quite broadly. He just said to me, "I told you I would sort that old ogre out, and I did". To this day I don't know how he did it, but I later met his son, who was quite high up in the local NSDAP administration. He shook my hand and promised me there would be no repeat of my landlord's poor attitude.

The following week I was told of a small factory unit which had been set up in some woodland on the outskirts of

Mannheim. I was told there was work available for me and all I would have to do is go to the factory with my papers and sign up. I went there the following week on my old bicycle so I could gauge the distance from my home. It was almost forty minutes but was not an unpleasant ride. It was only a small production/finishing facility with a staff of thirty young women. I say 'young women'; one of them was an older woman I thought to be around sixty years of age. She had her two front teeth missing and whenever she spoke she would shower you with saliva. The youngest there was a seventeen-year-old girl they nicknamed Baby. I was shown what I would be doing, which was packing 2-cm ammunition into wooden crates. Then I was shown where to go in an emergency. There was this underground concrete shelter with a large reinforced metal door. The shelter was nearly forty feet deep and so was quite safe from bombs. While I was shown around my paperwork was issued so I could start work the following morning. It was an early start at 6am and I was told not to be late.

I cycled home feeling a little better, though my thoughts soon drifted back to those of my dear husband. I wondered if I would ever hear anything from him and how he was being treated by those who had captured him. I had heard that the Russians were brutal towards captured German prisoners and felt slightly melancholy. When I arrived home I went and told my neighbour about my job at the factory and he was very happy for me. He did remark that it was ironic that man had started this war and that women now had to pick up many of the pieces as a result. I left my neighbour's home then went straight to bed, hoping to get as much sleep as possible, ready for the next morning.

I was awake before dawn next morning and a thick mist carpeted the town, especially over the river. I set off on my bicycle, arriving at the little factory fifteen minutes early. Some of the women were outside smoking cigarettes, others just milled about waiting for the evening shift to come off duty. As the evening shift walked wearily out of the factory door, their faces stained with what looked like soot, I felt a pang of nervousness. That's when the girl they called Baby walked up and took me by the arm and said "come on, I'll show you in." We went in and I was again given a safety brief on what to do in the event of an air raid alarm or fire within the factory etc. Everyone knew what they had to do in an emergency.

The women I worked with were a mixed bunch for sure. Some would talk openly with you about all kinds of things. One used to discuss her sexual antics of the previous night with her boyfriend. She would go into so much detail the other women would laugh and shake their heads in disbelief. I would grab Baby and cover her ears with my hands. She would be trying to pull my hands away, terrified of missing any of the conversation. Baby was my favourite workmate and we even arranged to meet up outside work on our days off. All I remember is that her name was Elle and she lived at home with her mother and father. We would have Sundays off and we used to go for little walks or to the cinema in Heidelberg to catch up on the latest news. Of course it soon dawned on us both that it was bullshit. One morning we all turned up for work as usual and Baby asked me if I would swap my shifts with her. She had been allocated an evening shift, which she did not want to do, so I volunteered to cover. Baby would do my day shift the next day and I would do her evening shift. As we finished work we hugged and I told her I would see her the next day. I told her she owed me a favour for this. She shouted back, "I will buy you coffee on Sunday, Hilde."

The next day had been lively due to much enemy action in the air. Several raids had passed over Heidelberg on their way to bomb industrial targets in Mannheim and Ludwigshafen. I spent most of the day trying to sleep, but what with air raid warnings and the distant thud of bombs going off it was somewhat difficult to relax. It was a relief with the approach of late afternoon. I had a small cup of coffee and then jumped on my bicycle just as it was getting dark. It was an uneventful journey yet quite pleasant, with the tree-lined country lanes offering a sense of security even if they were very dark. I was stopped a couple of times and asked to show my papers [...]. As I approached the woods where the factory was situated I noticed the orange and yellow glow of fire up ahead. There was a road block in place and I was told that I could go no further. I said I needed to get to work and was asked if it was at the small ammunition factory. I told the checkpoint soldiers yes it was and they should let me through or I would be disciplined for being late for my shift. One of them dropped his head and, almost in a whisper, told me, "That factory was hit earlier in the afternoon. [...] Two five-hundred-pound high explosives fell on it [...] There are no survivors." I felt numb at the words as they began to impact on me. I sank to the ground feeling sick. I asked, "Are you sure there were no survivors?" The soldiers nodded their heads. I just began to cry. All my friends were dead inside that inferno. I thought of Baby lying in there, dead, at just seventeen. I wanted to go to the site but fire crews were busy fighting the blaze and there was the danger still from exploding ammunition. I just thought this is it, it's over.

I had to be helped to my feet and even then I couldn't stand up without assistance. My bicycle was placed in the back of a Luftwaffe truck and I was given a ride home. My elderly neighbour watched as the truck pulled up and my bike was unloaded. He was concerned and came out to see if everything was alright. One of the soldiers explained what had happened and my neighbour insisted I stay with him and his wife that evening. I spent the next week trying to recover. I couldn't accept that Baby was gone and it was like some bad dream. My moods became increasingly worse as the weeks passed. It got to the point where my doctor summoned my parents and told them I needed to go into a sanatorium or my health would suffer further. I had experienced what amounted to a nervous breakdown.

By 1944 German industry was experiencing the full fury of the Allied strategic bombing campaign, but those working in the various factories at the time proved remarkably resilient. Despite the death and destruction raining down upon them, many of the weapons and munitions plants were up and running again just hours after being bombed. Diana Richter recalled:

> It was a simple case of the area being checked for any unexploded bombs. Then rubble was moved out of the way, along with any corpses and body parts, and production would start up again. Often, we worked in close proximity to unexploded bombs. There was one which I recall being trapped in metal girders in the roof of one of the factory units. There was no way it could be taken down so we had to work with it up there.

Many factory units which were considered essential to the German war effort were moved to underground facilities. Many of these underground facilities had been constructed by slave labourers. One such infamous underground factory was in the southwest of Niedersachswerfen, at a place known as Kohnstein. Originally a gypsum mine, the maze of deep underground tunnels created by mining provided a perfect manufacturing facility for the V-2 rocket programme. Kira Runstedt was a twenty-one-year-old nurse employed at the facility, catering for the medical needs of the German workers and specialists employed there. In a very rare interview with Kira, which took place via a phone call back in 2003, I was able to document one German woman's experiences of the Kohnstein plant. It was pretty clear she had mixed emotions regarding her past yet her memory was as vivid as that of a youngster. Kira recalled:

> I arrived at the Kohnstein in mid-1943, just one of a group of young German girls who had completed medical school. We lived not far from the Kohnstein underground factory. They always needed good medics and nurses there due to the many dangerous activities being conducted. Our services were exclusively for the German workers and not for the benefit of the many slave labourers who were brought in […]. I was attracted by the pay, which was better than I could have got working in a hospital. I had extensive dental experience too, so could perform two roles when required. I did not get to see the entire underground factory, but I was given a

kind of a tour around certain areas. I saw components being manufactured for the V-2 missiles. These required specialist workers, though some slave labourers with the necessary knowledge were brought in from the occupied countries. If a slave worker sliced his hands or arms to the bone then one of his own would bandage it up and he would be forced to continue working. If one of our German workers did the same he would receive the best possible treatment and given rest. I recall one young man who had slipped with a piece of razor-sharp steel. The wound looked as if it had been made with a surgical scalpel. You could see the bones in his fingers. I cleaned, disinfected and then sutured the wounds and bandaged his hand, putting it in a sling. He was sent home to recuperate.

I saw the slave workers who were brought in, mainly from the east. They were literally worked to death. They worked all day, and sometimes all night, without rest, food or water. Those who died were removed by other slave workers and thrown in a pit outside. By the end of the war there were many corpses rotting on the hillside. The food supplied to the slave workers was anything but nutritious. It was a thin, brown-coloured soup which resembled faecal matter but minus the lumps. I recall many of the slave workers having these cuts and other wounds on their bodies. Some of the wounds had formed thick scabs. One was so hungry that he often sat and picked off the scabs of his wounds and ate them. Anything to feel something in his stomach I guess it was better than nothing. I managed to speak with him once. He was from Poland; an engineer by trade, which is why he was brought to work here. I saw this man – who I thought would have been in his forties – a few times afterwards. It was difficult to get close enough to talk to him. I found a way around this by pretending I was mocking and abusing him. Instead, I threw him a small handkerchief containing a small amount of bread, cheese and sausage. I did feel terrible for these people. My father used to say, "You must not get emotionally attached or emotionally involved; this is dangerous for you and for us." We fled the factory before the end of the war and I made my way home, which took me twelve days as I travelled on foot. Most of the earnings made during my employment at Kohnstein were sent home to my mother and father.

Danni Foestahl had continued to work as much as she could, despite the disruption caused by the Allied bombing of the city of Emden throughout 1944. The knockout blow on the city – 6 September 1944 – was yet to come. Danni recalls:

I still had my apartment, which I felt was safe as it was it was out of the way of anything the bombers might go after. We still had to run to air raid shelters frequently due to the bombing attacks that were taking place day and night. My boyfriend had moved in with me and my pet daschund. With the way things were at the time he began to get on my nerves. I needed money and was doing any work I could find, including some voluntary work I was asked to do. He went out to work, but on many occasions I would arrive home to find he had finished long before me. We began to argue and the relationship was just not the same. The spark had gone and we stopped making love and generally we began to resent each other. The last straw came when he started picking on my dog. He never physically did anything, but he would sit there making horrible remarks. We were having lunch one day and he said, "Why does that fucking dog of yours keep trying to eat its own anus?" He was of course referring to the dog licking himself, as dogs do. I just stood up and shouted, "Oh, just get out of here. Go on, get out, and don't come back." He gathered the few things he had brought with him when he moved in with me and he left. Then it was just me and my little dog, and the war around us.

Some men used to make me really fucking sick. I would be out all day, popping back and forth to see my dog was okay. Then I would get home, cook something for us to eat, and have a bath, if I was lucky. Then he would have no understanding as to why I was not in the mood for fucking his brains out. All that they seemed to want was sex, sex, and more sex from you. Hitler had created this [...] male-dominated society where feminism was supposed to cower in corners. When a man demanded he wanted to fuck you, you had to just lie down and let him do it. Sorry, but that is not the view that I shared.

I was so tired and drained. Once I was cutting one of my regular clients' hair and almost cut off a piece of skin of my little finger. It was a near disaster as my blood poured into the woman's hair and all over the place. She was very good though and assured me it had not put her off. Even in this war women still wanted to try their best to look good, have their hair cut and look pretty.

We still had to buy things we needed and we could not do that if we had no money. We still had to survive by working and producing what food we could ourselves. I had a small vegetable garden, which helped me out. I mostly made soups from the vegetables. It was a little bland but it all helped. I was becoming concerned about the way the war was going. They were telling us "It will be okay, we will prevail" and things like that. Yet how could you take comfort from their words when you had enemy aircraft in the skies above you day and night, and whispers of the Red Army defeating our armies in the east? Oh yes, I heard many whispers, and one young woman said to me once, "It's so hard keeping the wolf from the door, yet bigger wolves are coming." The fairy tales about wolves and other sinister creatures were typical of German folklore. We were told the stories from little children and often used them when referring to actual situations.

Chapter 10

Eintopf Kotzen (One-pot Puke)

The question of food rationing was something that had haunted Hitler from the moment that he had committed Nazi Germany to waging war with the world. Hitler clearly understood how food rationing during the First World War had severely affected German morale and had been a contributory factor in their defeat. The rationing of food in Germany during the Second World War only became a consideration in mid-to-late 1943. The Nazi invasion of the Soviet Union, which began in 1941, meant that captured resources could be transported back to Germany to augment supplies at home. There was an abundance of food, including cereal crops, fruits and vegetables, which were then sent back to Germany, usually by rail. However, as the Red Army began to push the Germans back from captured territories in the east those food resources were lost.

The Allied bombing campaign also had a detrimental effect upon domestic productivity in Germany, while the British navy prevented food supplies reaching Germany by sea. Though locally produced fruit and vegetables were plentiful, their distribution around the country was severely disrupted by Allied bombing and fighter bomber activity. The rail network was the only viable way of transporting food and other goods from the rural areas to where they were needed in the towns and cities. The Allied commanders understood how vital the German rail links were to her war effort and concerted efforts were made to destroy them. In the cities if shops were not destroyed by the bombing they were often empty of anything to sell.

As a result, rationing of some basic foods had to be implemented. The system adopted in Nazi Germany was very similar to that in place in Britain and favoured those working in the heavy industries. These workers were allocated more rations than, for example, a farm labourer, policeman or shop worker. Helena Koerg found herself struggling very badly with her three girls in early 1944. The two younger ones, Helga and Ilsa, complained of constantly being hungry. Helena recalled:

> I had to send them to bed and tell them to try not to run around and use up energy. That way they would not feel so hungry. Gertrud was a true saviour yet again. She would go out with her friends from the BDM and they would come back with any fruits or vegetables that were in season. Where they had got them from I never asked [she laughs]. One afternoon they came back with a handful of small sachets of coffee and a half-full jar of fruit jam. I gave the jam to Helga and Ilse and they ate it all between them. The coffee was like finding gold as it was not available by this time. Looking at the packets I soon noticed they had come from army rations. Gertrud later told me that she and her friends from the BDM had visited an army training camp. They had climbed the fence surrounding it and begun searching around, and that is where they found the items. [...]
>
> They planned to go back and do another search the next day. I told Gertrud to be careful and if there were any soldiers there they must not try and enter the camp. The following day they went off and were late coming back. When they did come back they were covered in dust and grime. One of the girls had lost her shoes and was standing in her white socks. I asked her, "Where are your shoes?" and she explained she had kicked them off in a panic as they were climbing the fence to leave the camp. They had been spotted and chased off by a man guarding the camp. He even fired several shots in the air. They did, however, have a small bag containing more small pouches of coffee and sugar. I begged the girls to not go back there. If they get caught we would all be in serious trouble. The authorities would class it as common burglary, which was a criminal act, considering the circumstances the country was in. The girls agreed to not go back. One of them then said, "There are more camps around here than that one so we will go and look at those." The girls also helped dig up a portion of our back yard so we could grow some vegetables. People started

growing potatoes and things, anywhere there was spare soil or ground to do it. Every bit helped us survive as the rationing was quite severe.

Gertrud also remembers raiding the army training camps with her friends from the BDM:

Oh, it was great fun and very exciting back then as we were teenage girls. We were not scared at all. The thought of finding something sweet overruled the fear of being caught. I did not look at it as stealing, as much of what we found had been left behind by soldiers in training. When we got chased one time this man fired shots in the air with a pistol. One of my friends was struggling to get over the wire fence and she had to kick her shoes off. That was not good as she had to walk home afterwards in just her socks and explain to her mother why she lost her shoes. Clothing and footwear was not easy to replace at that time, but she had her boots, which BDM girls could buy, so she wore them afterwards all the time. We had many exciting times as school had to be abandoned, and we had these air raids coming in which were exciting to watch, though very dangerous. If we were out and a raid sounded we dashed to the nearest shelter. We knew where they were so felt quite safe.

Ursula Bomme remembers the rationing and the drastic measures some families take in order to feed themselves:

My father made traps and he tried several versions to try and catch birds and things. He was unsuccessful many times and he would come in grumbling about it. I remember him hanging these nets up in the trees around the house. For some days the nets didn't catch anything, then the one morning there was a pigeon tangled up in the net. He ran out like an excited child and pulled the net down from the tree. He grabbed the bird and twisted its neck to kill it. He then pulled out all of the feathers and cut out the guts. It was not pleasant to see this being done, but when he had finished he held up the carcass in jubilation that we would have some meat to go in the *Eintopf Kotzen* [One-pot Puke]. This was the nickname he gave to the one-pot meals brought in due to the rationing situation.

The one-pot meal idea was nothing new, having been introduced into German homes from 1933. Traditionally, German families ate a similar Sunday roast dinner to the one enjoyed by British families. During the mid-1930s German housewives were encouraged to replace their traditional Sunday roast on the first Sunday of every month. The savings made were then donated to the *Winterhilfswerk*, a Nazi-run charity established to feed and clothe the poor through the winter months. When the Second World War broke out the one-pot meal was considered something of a common sacrifice towards a common purpose. There were many Germans who despised the one-pot meal, but with the onset of rationing it became one of the primary sources of nourishment in Nazi Germany.

Eintopf recipes consisted of homegrown root vegetables, fruit and meat, when available. As the war progressed, though, meat became scarce. Ursula Bomme continues:

Sometimes we could obtain a few scraps of beef or pork from the butcher. The meat scraps were added to the vegetables and this created a kind of stew. As vegetables were still plentiful, a large pot could be cooked up, which would feed a family for a few days. When it was all gone another pot would be cooked up. My father became irritated by the lack of meat so he tried trapping his own. Pigeons were always plentiful and he became very good at catching them in nets in the trees. When added to the stew they actually tasted very good and added much flavour to the otherwise mundane vegetable slop. They all used to say, "We are following the Führer's example and eating only vegetables," yet eating vegetable stews every day soon becomes very boring. My father would put any birds he caught in the net into the one-pot meals. Sometimes he would catch sparrows and they would end up in the pot. The only birds you could not eat were carrion feeders such as crows. Crow's meat would make you sick if you ate it, they used to say, as crows feed off dead animals. Due to the bombing it was not uncommon to see crows pecking at corpses buried in rubble piles. So eating those was definitely not a good idea. My father also once caught someone's cat and that ended up in the cooking pot. I was not told about it until after I had eaten it. Father had told me it was a rabbit. When I learned the truth I almost vomited. I recall my father laughing at me and telling me I was much too sensitive considering we are a nation deep in a war.

Helena Koerg recalled the one-pot meals:

The only good thing about them was that you could throw anything in them. Carrots, potatoes, cabbage, onions and peas; anything at all edible could be thrown into these stews. If you were careful a big pot would feed a small family for nearly seven days. When I could get them, I often added sausage scraps to the stew. By 1944 meat was becoming harder to obtain and we often had to make do with meals containing no meat at all. The men often complained that the diet of vegetables made their bowel movements too runny. I remember an old neighbour saying once that one of his friends farted and had messed himself as a result of the diet.

Gertrud Koerg also remembers the one-pot meal and recalls:

They were just plain vegetable stews most of the time. We didn't really mind it though as we were raised on them. We used to have a roast meal on a Sunday, but that was before the war really began to affect our lives. In the *Jungmadelbund* and *Bund Deutscher Madel* they cooked large pots of stew so it was nothing new for us to have to adapt to. I know some of the girls in the BDM called these stew dinners "shit". You couldn't let anyone hear you say that though as it was said these stews were Hitler's idea at solving the nation's food problems. Some of them did taste like shit, I agree [she laughs], but it was something and it kept you going. My younger sisters struggled some days with the lack of food. My mother would make them lie down to try and conserve their energy. By doing so they might feel less hungry.

Ilsa and Helga Koerg certainly did have an entirely different opinion to that of their mother and elder sister. Ilsa continues:

Me and Helga hated those stews. We had to force ourselves to swallow every revolting spoonful. Our mother was a beautiful cook but we were kids and most kids hate vegetables. So these stews we had to eat were a kid's nightmare [she laughs]. At night me and Helga would lie awake and talk about roast potatoes and roast pork and how we missed sausages. These once-common items were now virtually impossible to buy. There just was none available. There were black market operators who could source cuts of meat for you but the prices being asked were extortionate. Plus the fact black market trading was an offence and anyone caught selling goods or food on the black market could find themselves in serious trouble. Seasonal fruits were always a blessing as our mother would put all the fruits into the pot and boil them up. They were not always very sweet as we had virtually no sugar to spare for cooking. But the stewed fruit pots were far more welcome than the vegetable ones.

Ilse Koerg recalls the delivery of some baby rabbits to her grandparents' home one morning:

These sweet little rabbits arrived and I thought, oh, great, we have some animals as pets now. Grandpapa soon corrected me and said, "These are not for pets, my young lady, these will be for us to eat when they are big enough. They will grow fat on any scraps we can give them and, in time, we will have stew with meat for once in a long while." I was horrified by what grandpapa said but that was my childish perception of things at the time, I guess.

We saved up any vegetable waste and fed the rabbits on the scraps. The bunnies soon grew fat and then it was time to eat them. I kicked up such a fuss that, in the end, I was granted one of the rabbits to keep as a pet. I held the little rabbit close to my chest and promised I would look after it. Grandpapa just stood there with a puzzled but beaten expression on his face. He didn't have the heart to say no to me. The other poor bunnies were not as fortunate and had to go. I remember my grandpapa grabbing one rabbit by its back legs. It began to squeal and kick and try to escape, then he said, positioning his hand behind its neck just below its head, "You strike it hard, just here, and it will die instantly." Then he delivered it a heavy blow with his hand, like a karate chop. The rabbit convulsed for a few seconds, urinating as it did so, then lay quite still. He then asked grandma to pass him a sharp knife. I couldn't watch as he skinned and gutted the animal, and the smell was awful. I told him I could not eat that thing after seeing him do that. Grandma prepared the rabbit, with some vegetables, in a stew and it went into the oven to slowly cook. When it was ready I was still reluctant to eat some, but when I did try it was delicious and I soon ate all mine.

Horst Kopfel recalls the risks some went to in order to make money on the black market:

I knew of a group of men who went out at night into *Reichsmarschall* Hermann Göring's estate after his wild boar. It was an incredibly risky endeavour. Yet there were people, usually wealthy people, who were prepared to pay good money for a decent lump of pork. I know they spent a few days hiding out on Göring's forest estate. They came back with a male boar and two piglets. The piglets were cut into half and made good money. The boar was cut up into joints and not one part of the animal went to waste. Due to the risks involved, payment for the meat was taken in advance. I don't think Göring ever learned of the poaching going on right on his doorstep. Most of us were aware of the fact that the fat oaf was not eating those rotten one-pot meals himself. He was eating very well while the rest of the nation had to exist on shit.

Many of the leading figures in the Third Reich were still living their opulent lifestyles, despite the hardships and privations faced by ordinary people. Martin Bormann, Joachim von Ribbentrop, Heinrich Himmler and Joseph Goebbels, along with many in the Nazi Officer elite, were still enjoying the privileged lifestyle thanks to their loyalty to Hitler. Nineteen-year-old Elizabeth Schwin worked as a maid for the foreign minister, von Ribbentrop, briefly in 1944 and revelled in the extravagance of her boss:

> He often hosted these large dinner parties with the finest foods and wines, spirits and champagne. It amazed me that he had all of this while the rest of us ate stew most days. These big men in the Nazi elite were certainly not leading by example. They were detached from the ordinary people in every conceivable way. Von Ribbentrop even had expensive handmade chocolate liqueurs, which were handed around to his guests after a meal. I recall seeing them and thinking to myself, when was the last time I had tasted chocolate? You could not help yourself to any of these things as Ribbentrop was so mean he would actually count the chocolates that were left. If you took any he would know. I was told most of those left were thrown away rather than offered to his staff. I just found it all very difficult to take in. On the one hand the Nazis were preaching that we were an equal society, all fighting for the same goal, yet on the other hand there were still these class divisions of the haves and have nots. To me that kind of arrogance made little sense. National Socialism was as fake as any other political ideology.

Lisa Schauer from Munich recalled how groups of young men and women would head out into the countryside around their towns and cities to gather fruits, nuts and hunt for rabbits or birds:

> I remember in the May of 1944, one fine Sunday afternoon, there was me my two younger brothers and sister and

ten other local girls and boys. We headed out into the countryside to forage for things we could eat. We had to stay away from open fields for safety reasons and made our way up through the woodlands wherever possible. As I was the oldest of the gang, at twenty-three, I would lead the way. We carried old grain sacks with us to put anything we found in. My brothers and sister were very excited at the prospect of finding additional treasures such as field mushrooms and nuts. As we walked through the fields we often passed anti-aircraft gun crews. We would stop and talk to them. The boys would ask them about how many kills they had made, and ask questions about the guns. The flak crews were quite nice and would point out where they had seen nuts growing on the trees and bushes. We actually found quite a bounty and soon our bags were filled with apples, berries, mushrooms and nuts.

On the way back home one of the boys spotted a bee nest hanging from a branch up in a tree. He had the idea we could knock it down and see if there was any honey inside. I told them it was a stupid idea and that they would end up being stung for their trouble. They wouldn't listen and so, from what we felt was a safe distance, we sat down munching on some apples to watch the show. The Hitler Youth boys did show great resourcefulness and threw sticks at the bee nest to try to dislodge it from the tree. They threw a heavy stick in a boomerang fashion and scored several hits on the nest. The angry bees started to come out and filled the air with that characteristic buzzing sound. My younger sister said to me, "How many bees do you think are in that nest?" I replied, "Hundreds, maybe even a thousand. I don't know for sure." One of the boys had a catapult and he was looking for a suitable missile to launch at the nest, which was proving stubborn for them to dislodge. He managed to find some stones, and after selecting one he placed it in the leather cup of the catapult. We watched as he drew back the elastic, taking careful aim at the nest. He looked like some medieval archer about to launch an arrow. As he released his grip on the elastic the stone made a shriek as it hurtled towards its target. He scored a bullseye and the bees nest fell to the ground with a crash, releasing a cloud of very angry stingers. My brothers and sister dropped their apples in horror as the cloud of insects gathered momentum and began searching out the source of the disturbance. We got up and ran like our arses were on fire through the trees. We could hear all the commotion going on behind us. The boys were shouting and squawking in terror as they too fled the angry insects.

We ran for some distance then stopped and waited for the others to come. One by one they came into view along the woodland path, out of breath and red in the face. I asked if any of them were stung and all replied that they hadn't been stung and were all okay. We all stood there and laughed about it. One of the boys then said, "Well, what do we do now? What about all that honey we have left behind there." We decided we would sit down and wait and then go back later and see if the bees were still around their nest. If they had gone we would put the nest in one of the sacks and take it home. It might need smoking to drive any remaining bees away, but I was sure my father could do this in return for some honey. The problem was that no one wanted to go back and risk being attacked by the bees. So I said I would go back and have a look but I would take the greater share of honey for doing so. I walked back along the track through the trees and could see the nest lying on the ground. There were a few bees around but didn't seem to be enough to pose any threat to me. I opened the grain sack and rolled the nest into it with a stick. I then walked back to the others in triumph.

We stopped to talk with the flak gunners again on the way back home. They jokingly asked us if we had had a successful hunting trip. [...] One guy asked me, "What have you got in there?" pointing to the sack I was carrying. I told them it was honey and opened up the sack to show them. As I did, several angry bees flew out of the bag and immediately began to attack. The flak gunners were flapping around, waving their arms to stop the bees from stinging them. They ended up jumping over the sandbag perimeter around their position and running a short distance away. The bees buzzed around angrily for some minutes before flying off. One of the flak gunners commented, "What if there had been an alert right at that moment? We would have been well and truly fucked, wouldn't we?" We all laughed and then headed off home. On our way one of the boys climbed up a tree to get to a bird's nest. There were three small eggs in the nest. He took them out and climbed back down. He then bit into one of the eggs. It was rancid and he quickly spat the contents out of his mouth. We all laughed at him as he was bent over trying to vomit. It was a walk of nearly six miles and by the time we arrived home it was almost dusk. We dropped the sacks in the woodshed and shut the door and went inside the kitchen where our mother was cooking. Yes, you guessed it; a one-pot stew.

Alessa Goberg recalls the hardships of 1944 and the one-pot meals:

On the farms in the countryside we fared better than those who lived in the urban areas. We could shoot rabbits and any other animals on our land. We did our best to grow what crops and vegetables we could on our land. We actually grew enough to feed people. The only problem was transporting the food out of the farms. It became incredibly dangerous for goods trains to operate. If they attempted to move in daylight they were attacked by enemy planes. I actually saw this happen on more than one occasion. People were killed and the goods being transported ruined. Attempts were made to move goods by rail at night, but damage to tracks and infrastructure caused considerable delays. We even tried moving things by using horses and carts but even these would be attacked without any mercy by our enemy. We tried using horse-drawn carts at night but the distances involved were just too great, even if we transported in this way in a relay fashion. We would have to sit out the daylight hours in the woods and return home in the dark. Due to these problems it was just impossible to get food supplies out from the rural areas into the cities.

Even on the farms we were encouraged to be thrifty and live on vegetable and fruit stews. The one-pot stews were not new to me. There were many times we had to exist on them in the past: if we'd had bad crops one year and certain things were in short supply. These one-pot stews were regarded as a national dish, especially in times of trouble when food became scarce. Rabbits were always plentiful on our land, along with various woodland birds. Some of the young rabbits would be caught live and sent to families in towns and cities. You would try and get males and females so they could be bred. Rabbit meat was wonderful and there would be little waste. Even the offal would go into the stews. I knew that in the cities there were people who had to contend with eating watery cabbage or potato stews with no meat at all. Boar was also common on our land, but we only ever hunted them when they were not in the mating season or giving birth to young.

There were desperate people who came out from the cities to try and poach animals from our land. By 1944 most of the poachers were actually young women like me. We were instructed by the local authorities that, if we caught anyone taking animals from our land, they should be held at gunpoint and the local police called. Order had to be maintained to preserve the dignity and wellbeing of the nation, we were told. There was one night that I caught two young women and a boy with one of our chickens. They had already killed it by the time I discovered them, but its squawks had alerted the whole house to their presence. I grabbed my father's rifle, loaded and cocked it, and went outside with my brother, who held a lamp for me so I could see. We chased the people for some distance in the dark until they suddenly stopped, dropped the chicken, and stood with their hands in the air in surrender. When we shone the light on them and saw their wretched state I just felt so sorry for them. They were desperate people. The women explained that their men were fighting for Germany in the war and they did not have enough food. We questioned them briefly about where they had come from and then told them to go on their way and that we would say nothing to the police about it. As they walked off I shouted to them, "Here, you forgot this," and picked up the chicken and held it up. One woman came back, took the chicken from me, and said "thank you". They then disappeared into the night. I never saw them again and I could never have held them hostage and handed them over to the authorities. When we returned to the house me and my brother both agreed to say that we had lost the poachers in the dark. We did not like having to tell lies but felt in this case it was justified. I remember saying to my brother, "This is not good. People are becoming hungry and desperate. It is only a matter of time now."

We saw the enemy planes over our fields in the daytime and we heard the drone of their engines at night as we lay in our beds. The distant rumble of bombs going off through the night was commonplace. I thought of those poor bastards who were being bombed […]. I was feeling very concerned and no longer inclined to believe in some form of divine deliverance. Hitler was kidding many people, but if you actually stopped to think, you could see we were not winning any war; we were losing it.

Chapter 11

A Nation's Pain

Tuesday, 6 June 1944 saw the beginning of the Allied liberation of Nazi-occupied Western Europe. The initial assault phase of Operation Overlord was known as Operation Neptune. It began on D-Day, 6 June 1944, and ended on 30 June 1944, by which time the Western Allies had gained a secure foothold in Normandy. Operation Overlord had been no easy undertaking. It was one of the largest seaborne invasions in military history. Allied casualties during the initial landing phase – with the exception of the American landings at Omaha Beach – had proved relatively light considering the sheer scale of the operation. Overlord suffered setbacks but proved a success. A long road still lay ahead for the Allies, however, and they understood clearly that victory would have to be paid for in the blood of both sides.

As the Allied invasion was taking place Adolf Hitler had been sleeping. No one dared disturb the Führer as many were of the opinion that Normandy was a decoy to draw German forces away from the actual invasion, which would take place in the Calais area. By the time Hitler had woken to the news, it became clear to the German High Command that Normandy was indeed the full-scale invasion. Reports coming in were far from good, yet Hitler was still convinced of securing victory. The ever-increasing cocktail of narcotics he was consuming almost certainly had an effect on his judgement. He was by this time incapable of making any rational military decisions. He was arguing constantly with his generals and exhibiting signs of psychosis. He was a leader hell-bent on the destruction of his own nation. There would be no miraculous victory, only misery, especially for the people in the towns, cities and villages of Germany.

On receipt of the news of the Allied foothold in Normandy, Helena Koerg wrote in her diary:

> It is as I had feared. It is like a bad dream that you do not want to believe is actually reality. From the moment the

Americans became involved in this war I felt we were all doomed to failure. There is much talk of a miracle weapon which will drive the enemy back into the sea. They are saying in the streets, "the Führer will prevail and we must follow him to victory." We have suffered some terrible bombings of our city. The defiance of the people here is admirable. Rather than leave they simply move away from the centre of the city. They pick themselves up and try to continue. Many have left Kassel now, saying it's too dangerous to stay here. I am frightened for the girls and I have received news from Reinhard that we should leave the city and head out into the countryside. There are many camps being organized outside of the city for people who have lost their homes or are in danger. We are torn between wanting to stay in our homes and a subterranean lifestyle of hiding from the bombs under the ground in shelters or cellars. We have grown accustomed to this way of life. It is not easy but we have little choice.

Tragedy would surface for the Koerg family when, in July 1944, Helena received news that her husband, Reinhard, had been seriously injured. The news came as a terrible blow to Helena and her family, but there was now some hope that Reinhard would return at least alive from his war service. Helena was somewhat mystified as to how her husband had been badly injured as he had been working with a medical team behind the battlefront. When she began to make enquiries as to the nature of her husband's wounds and the circumstances surrounding them the information she was given was not very helpful. She was told that Reinhard's injuries had been caused by artillery fire. Everything that could be done to treat him was being done and she would receive further news on her husband in due course. Helena wrote in her diary:

I don't know what to think or how to break this news to the girls. I have decided we are leaving and will walk to my mother and father's as soon as it is light in the morning. I cannot deal with this alone. I can feel my spirits slipping away into a pit of darkness. I cannot eat, I cannot sleep, and all I want to do is cry. The other women say, "Helena, it will all be alright. Please don't worry." I do not share their optimism, and now Reinhard has been badly hurt.

They won't say exactly what his injuries are, or whether he can walk, or whether he is crippled, or anything. It is driving me insane not knowing what condition the man I love and adore is in at this time.

Gertrud Koerg recalls the news of her father being broken to her:

It was shattering for us, that is all I can say. My mother got us up before dawn on a warm July morning and told us we are going to grandma and grandpapa's. As we left our house […] I recall looking back and feeling like I would never see home again. We made the two-hour journey on foot. We passed scenes that would not have been out of place in a horror film. Carts filled with dead bodies. I recall the face of a little girl on the back of one of the carts. She was dead and her skin looked grey, yet her eyes were wide open and staring, as if still alive and trapped in the moment of terror just prior to her death. These were common sights by that time. As we neared our grandparents home there were some berry trees and we stopped and ate some of the berries. We had not eaten for two days so we were all very hungry.

Our grandparents went berserk when they saw us. They remarked on the state of us and mother began to cry. Our grandmother took us out into the kitchen and gave us some bread and stew they had left from the previous evening. As we sat and bolted down the bread and stew, I could hear grandpapa shouting, "No, no! This cannot be right." After we had eaten we were called back into the living room where I could see my mother being comforted by our grandmother. We sat down and I cuddled my two sisters close to me as grandpapa said to us, "Your dear daddy is not well. He has been hurt, but he will be alright. He will be back home soon." We all cried and began babbling and asking questions as to what happened to our father and when he will be home and things like that. My grandmother made the big double bed for us and we climbed into it and tried to sleep. My sisters cried for a while but fell asleep due to the stresses of the day. We just wanted news on father now […].

It was a bitterly cruel twist of fate that less than one week after receiving the news of her husband being badly injured Helena received news that Reinhard had died from complications resulting from his injuries. Gertrud Koerg recalls that day:

> When the news was broken to us I just went completely numb. I began to tremble and my heart raced. We all just cried together. We didn't know how to go on from this. We had a lot of support from friends of our grandparents and old friends of our mother who still lived nearby. Grandmother was concerned about mother and told me, "You must do as much as you can now for your little sisters. They are going to need you to be strong for them. Your mother is not coping well with any of this. If only I was not so damned old I could do more." I understood what she was trying to say to me. I couldn't grieve as the others grieved; I had to hide it all and be the strong one through all of this. Maybe this will all be over soon, I thought to myself. Maybe then we can try to pick up the pieces of our lives and return to normality. My father's face was constantly on my mind. Whenever I tried to sleep at night I could see him smiling at me in the darkness. I would reach out to him, but then his smiling face would vanish, leaving just the darkness again.

In a letter that was later forwarded to Helena Koerg, from Reinhard's commanding officer, Karl Herbert Litsch, he gave an explanation of the circumstances of Reinhard's death. It outlined a few facts, including how Russian long-range artillery was now targeting the German rear areas. They had fallen back several miles from the battlefront and felt they could continue their work there in relative safety. However, conditions soon made this impractical. Men were dying due to the field hospitals being too far behind the lines. Transport had been disrupted and the medical staff made their own decision to return to their former positions. Reinhard was initially badly wounded when two artillery shells landed near their tent. It was stated that he had suffered a double amputation. Both legs had been so badly mutilated by shrapnel that a surgeon had to remove them. The aftercare and treatment given was excellent and Reinhard had been expected to make a recovery, but his condition began to deteriorate after three days due to an infection. They were unable to move him until his condition stabilised and he lost consciousness and died shortly after. The letter also stated that he had been recommended for the War Merit Cross. The letter closed with the words: "It was a true honour to have known your husband, who I came to like and respect as a loyal servant of the Reich, despite all of the difficulties and dangers encountered. The fact that many men wounded are still alive is a lasting tribute to the memory of your husband and the steadfastness of the work which he had carried out in the service of our country."

The letter was cold comfort for Helena and she sat in stunned silence for some minutes, seemingly lost deep within her own thoughts. Gertrud recalls:

Mother would just sit and stare out of the window for hours on end. I could tell she had been crying, probably for hours. She had stopped working at the Henschel factory and was ordered to take rest. It seemed that at that moment in time we had lost our mother. The grief of losing father had destroyed her. She was like the bombed buildings we had lived around. The structures were often still standing but inside there was nothing left. That's what our mother was like at that time. I would try and talk with her and she would smile and hold my hands and caress my fingers. She would say, "What beautiful hands you have, Gertrud." She would still just mainly sit staring out of the window of our grandparent's home. I think she gained comfort from watching the flowers and the birds. Often these would be drowned out by those wretched enemy planes as they flew in to bomb Kassel again and again. What happened with our father hurt us beyond belief. It was the second family tragedy of that war. My friends in the BDM were tremendous. They did so much to help give us support and I received a lot of support as an individual from them too. It was my friends from the BDM who helped me through that dreadful time. If you were a BDM girl then every other BDM girl in Germany, whether you knew them or not, was a sister to you. We were bound by that sisterhood code. We looked after our people in need and ourselves.

Adelaine Seider's life was also touched by the cold embrace of a wartime tragedy in that summer of 1944:

Living in the Hitler Youth camps outside the city of Berlin was wonderful. We had quite a community there and it was all quite exciting at the time. This changed for me when an aunt of mine came to the camp to see me. I instinctively knew that something was wrong by the look on her face. She sat me down and told me that my mother and father had been lost. They were working in the factory when the warning was given of enemy planes. They were amongst the last people out of the factory […]. My aunt explained that my father kept looking at his watch, timing everything, saying, "We still have a few more minutes yet. We can finish this off first." One of the directors kept shouting at them to get out. When they finally ran out of the building the first bombs were already on their way down. My aunt said it was freak incident as a bomb had bounced off the ground and travelled several hundred yards before demolishing a wall. My mother and father had both been behind the wall at that point. I was told father died instantly but mother had survived for a few hours. My aunt told me she had been calling out my name then she died.

I became hysterical and had to be restrained. They forced some pills into my mouth and I don't recall much after that. They knocked me unconscious and when I woke up I felt like I had been sleeping for days, though it had only been about seven or eight hours. I felt strangely calm and was told I had to be sedated for my own good. My aunt was still by my side and I asked her, "Is it true or was all of that just a bad dream?" My aunt just shook her head and looked down at the floor. When I was well enough I went to live with my aunt and uncle. I did not want to leave the Hitler Youth camp. I felt safe there and made many new friends. My aunt was a lovely lady and my uncle was in the Luftwaffe and based locally. I just had to get used to living a new life now. I wanted to know when they were going to bury my mother and father but I was told this had already been done. When I asked questions my aunt became distressed and unable to talk about it. I would get told off for asking too many questions. I later heard they went into a mass pit somewhere. Most of the victims in that pit were bodies that were not in one piece. I reacted the same way as any normal child would. I cried at night and developed anxiety problems. I remember the BDM girls from the camp coming to visit me. They were always so nice and just came to see if I was alright.

Kitka Obermann had given birth to her second child, a little girl that she and Werner named Alice. The little girl was born in the midst of war, rationing and an uncertain future under Adolf Hitler's crumbling Reich.

Our daughter Alice was born at home and she was perfectly healthy, weighing 7lb. We were at Werner's parents' home, where we had our own space in which to live our lives. On a weekend I would take my son to see his father and he would stay at his father's often. We were as amicable as we could be with one another. I knew Joachim still had feelings for me as he would tell me so. He would keep asking me, "When are you coming back?" The hardest part was having to tell him I was not going back to him. We were just too different and too much had happened already for that to ever happen. I was totally in love with Werner and it was different altogether. Werner always wanted to be with me whereas Joachim was more in love with his work than me. There were other worries to contend with. The rationing, which had been introduced in 1943, severely limited what you could have and the amounts you could have. They gave you these ticket type things for bread, butter, milk, eggs and things. As I was a mother of two we did not do too badly, and we had enough to live on with the vegetables that Werner's parents had grown in their garden. Werner's mother had pickled vegetables and fruit stored in glass jars and had made jams too. With clothes you had to just make do with what you had, and you had to repair anything that ripped.

The social changes in Germany by 1944 were very concerning. There was this air of paranoia. People were really unsure as to whether Hitler was right or wrong for Germany now. Of course, people were unable to voice their discontent [...]. The dangers of speaking out were that you could be shot as a traitor or sent to a concentration camp as a non-believer. Old scores were being settled too. There were families informing on other families and fabricating lies about them purely out of hatred. The authorities had a nasty habit of always believing the liars, never the ones telling the truth. It was becoming a scary place to be, where you lived in fear of everything.

Danni Foestahl recalls what she refers to as the 'death of Emden':

One day stands out in my mind as one of the worst days of my life. It was Wednesday, 6 September 1944, when the enemy bombers literally wiped out the centre of our beautiful Emden. I was in my apartment with my dog when my neighbour was suddenly frantically banging on my door. When I opened the door my neighbour was saying in a frightened tone, "the bombers are coming we have to go to the shelter this instant." I told her not to panic as there were no targets near us, but we gathered the things we had ready for such an instance and went downstairs. Just a short distance away there was a residential shelter. Most of the locals had opted to stay in their homes, so when we arrived at the shelter there were only twelve other people there. My neighbour had heard the warning of an incoming raid on her small wireless set. It was a substantial enemy force and she felt a sense of unease so had to come to tell me. I told her she was being silly and it wouldn't be any worse than any of the other attacks on Emden. "We might not even get bombed," I can remember telling her.

The RAF bomber command force heading for Emden comprised 105 Halifax and 76 Lancaster bombers. The bombers were being escorted to the target by RAF Spitfires and USAAF P-51 Mustang fighters.

It would be the last RAF bombing raid on the city of Emden and would prove to be the most destructive. Danni Foestahl continues:

> We sat down inside the shelter and the air soon turned dank. It was like we were breathing in the breath of corpses. My dog began to bark as he could sense what was coming before it even reached us (as animals often can). I tried to keep him quiet but he continued to yap, yap, and yap. It had been barely twenty minutes since my neighbour came running to my door. There was that distinctive sound of flak guns then the rumble of engines in the sky above. The noise of the bombers grew in intensity to a kind of throbbing sound that strangely seemed to reverberate down through the shelter into your body. Then the bombs began to fall and we sat in silence. Even my dog stopped barking. He began to tremble and I cursed him as he urinated in my lap, the warm liquid soaking my thighs. The noise above was terrific as the bombs exploded. I remember saying, "What the hell are they doing up there? There is nothing of military significance to bomb. Why are they here dropping their bombs?" Nobody answered. They just sat with glum expressions of their faces. I knew from the noise above that this raid had been a big one. The bombs sounded much closer than the previous raids, and I could tell that civilian buildings would have been hit. We had to sit in that shelter and listen to the systematic destruction going on above.
>
> When the all clear was given we came out of the shelter and were shocked to see one of the worst sights I had ever seen. We could clearly see that Emden centre was gone. All that remained was a wall of fire. All of the historical buildings had gone and it soon transpired that those bastards had deliberately targeted the civilian population. Apparently this raid was in retaliation for the Luftwaffe attack on Coventry. The only historical buildings that survived the raid were an ancient wall erected in 1616 and a Gothic Church built in 1648. It was a nauseating scene. I saw people fleeing from the centre. I remember seeing women with their children and they were covered in what looked like black soot.

Some were carrying the bodies of their children in their arms. I recall one small child had all of the skin burned from its body. The mother was hysterical, but there was nothing anyone could do to save the child. The fires in the city were extensive and the fire fighting forces were doing their best, but I think they were overwhelmed. The fact that so much damage had been inflicted reflected the incompetence of our forces. The German military were unable to protect us from Allied air attacks. Those who emerged safely from air raid shelters and cellars after this raid asked the authorities "Where is the Luftwaffe?" I remember one young woman saying "Hermann Göering is a cow's vagina!" The truth was that nothing was going to save Germany now. You know, we just had that feeling that pretty soon it was all going to collapse like a broken wall.

Gunther Schalk was just twenty-three years old in September 1944. He had joined the Luftwaffe a year previously, training on the Messerschmitt Bf109G and Focke Wulf FW190A-8. Gunther recalled the criticism of the Luftwaffe's inability to defend German cities from the Allied bombing campaign.

Our problems were immense purely in terms of our trained and experienced manpower. We had enough fighter aircraft but too few pilots with the necessary experience to stay alive for any length of time. You soon learned the tricks of survival if you could stay alive for a few missions. In my first year of fighter operations I was shot down three times. On each occasion I bailed out uninjured. I was one of the very lucky ones. I was picked up and returned to my station within a few hours. I would receive a new aircraft then the next alert I would be in action once again. When we went into action we were outnumbered sometimes ten to one by P51s, P38s, Spitfires and P47s. The more experienced pilots would try and lure the fighters away while we attacked the bomber formations. Even with four heavy cannon the bombers were difficult to shoot down. Getting in close was not always easy and it was easy to open fire too soon and out of range so by the time you were within effective range you had used up most of your ammunition. It was a habit many of the new fighter pilots found hard to break.

When I went out for drinks in my uniform women would ask me questions like, "Where were you boys when the bombs were falling on us earlier?" and "Why aren't you shooting them down?" One day I told them, "We lost six pilots today trying to defend the city. One of them was just nineteen years old. We have no rest and are sometimes in the air for hours at a time in freezing temperatures. I am so tired that sometimes after landing my aircraft I am asleep in the cockpit before the propeller blades have even stopped turning. I am so worn out some days I have to be helped from my machine." I told them, "Don't you dare ever criticize me. I am doing all I can and many young men are being sacrificed pointlessly now in this war, which I can tell you now, we are not going to win." One had the nerve to shout "*Verrater*" [traitor] behind my back as I walked away. "Is this what our great race of people has come to?" I asked myself. At that point I felt I was fighting for nothing. I had a girlfriend living in Bonn. She was the only thing I thought about each time I climbed up into the cockpit of my aircraft. Would I ever see her again? Was this the last time I would ever climb up into the cockpit of my aircraft? I would ask myself "Will I die today in the flaming coffin of this Focke Wulf?" I would carefully place the small black-and-white photograph of my dearest Anna in the corner of the windscreen of my aircraft, say a prayer, and prepare for another battle.

Inge Sohn was a very pretty sixteen-year-old who had volunteered for the job of a telephone operator in the summer of 1944. She was the youngest of four siblings and recalled:

I had three older brothers, all of whom were serving in the military. One was serving in a flak regiment and the other two were both in the Luftwaffe, one a pilot the other ground crew working on maintenance. I was assisting with

Luftwaffe intelligence duties and became privy to all manner of conversations which passed through my department. I received mixed reactions from the men I worked with. Some would just sit staring at me from across the small office we worked in, while others would make remarks like, "You have no boyfriend or children as yet, young lady?" One of them always used to lean over me when I was working. He would pretend to be examining a document, but would lean right against me. It sometimes felt as if I had the devil himself breathing down the back of my neck. I knew what was on the minds of these men. They all wanted to walk me home after my day had finished. Where we lived we did not experience heavy bombing. The bombers flew over our little town on the way to Berlin and you would often see the dramas high up in the sky unfold as flak and fighters tried to stop them from dropping their bombs on the city.

I was late finishing one evening and was about to leave when this one young man offered to escort me home. I just thought "Oh no, here we go again," but let him walk me home. We were not far from my house when he insisted on stopping for a cigarette. He offered me one but as I didn't smoke I declined his offer. I stood awkwardly, leaning against a tree as he began to try and make funny small talk with me. He asked me if I had ever had a boyfriend, to which I replied "yes, but not at this time". Then he asked if I had ever been kissed properly. I did the kind of thing most young girls would have done, rolled my eyes and replied, "Yes, of course I have." I said to him, "Look, can we go now, it's getting late you know." Without a word he just grabbed hold of my hand and began stroking it. He was mumbling, "You have such beautiful, soft hands. Can I kiss them?" I told him not be so silly and pulled my hand away from him. There was a distant air raid alert and the sound of flak soon afterwards. He just said, "Look, watch the sky over there." In the direction he was pointing were little pops of yellow light and beams from searchlight batteries. It was an eerie kind of sight. The sound of the planes grew into a faint rumbling sound. I went to carry on walking home when

I was grabbed from behind and a hand put across my mouth. I tried to cry out, but couldn't. I was thrown down onto the ground and he was on top of me. I couldn't push him off. The sound of the planes was drowning out my screams for help. He was trying to kiss me and I kept thumping him on the back. With one hand he grabbed both my wrists, and using his full weight held my wrists above my head. With his free hand he was pulling down my underwear. I tried kicking but he was too big and strong for me. I knew exactly what was going to happen to me but could not believe it was happening. As he penetrated me he quickly changed his grip and with both his hands held my wrists down. He was staring down at me as he began raping me. I remember his face contorting in the twisted pleasure he was gaining from raping me. It was rough and it hurt because of the way he was holding me down. My shoulders felt as if they would pop out of their sockets. As he climaxed in me I stared into his eyes with defiance and hatred. When he got off me he acted as if nothing had even happened. He fastened his trousers and lit himself another cigarette. I got up, and as the noise of the planes began to fade, I said to him, "I hope you die, you filthy pig." He sneered at me, "It's your Reich duty to have babies, so what is your problem?" I shook my head at him and ran away in tears down the road. When I arrived home I washed myself out and prayed that this vile beast had not made me pregnant.

I never told anyone about the rape. I was terrified that if I tried to speak out he would say I was a liar and that I had consented to sex with him. He was twenty-six years old and knew people higher up in our offices. It would have been my word against his, wouldn't it? I kept quiet and I prayed that one day I would have the pleasure of seeing him die slowly for what he had done to me. The ironic thing is that not long after the end of the war he was diagnosed with an aggressive form of cancer. I wanted to go and see him and stare into his eyes, as he had done during the rape. I went to the hospital and told them I was a work colleague and they let me have a few minutes with him. He was deathly pale, almost grey in complexion. I whispered into his ear, "Does it hurt? Can you feel the disease eating you?" I'm not sure he even recognised me, but I stood before him looking into his eyes. I told him, "God is your judge," then I turned around and walked away. Less than a week later he was dead.

The pain of the rape lived with me for many years afterwards, as it does for victims of sexual attacks like this. Our society had become predatory towards its own females. The males resented the fact we could do anything they could do, within reason. I think him raping me was his way of reaffirming the male dominance thing. They felt that they could do what they wanted with you. As law and order slowly began to break down into the chaos brought about by the war, women became easy prey for certain individuals like that. Women and girls were the bearers of our nation's pain. It was us who would have to pay the price, pick up the pieces, and continue with life as if nothing had ever happened.

Chapter 12

Traitors Have no Grave

The relative happiness that Kitka Obermann had found with Werner Bothe would also be tainted by the war during the summer of 1944. Kitka, her son Roel, and newborn baby Alice were still living with Werner's parents in the large family home in Friedrichshafen. That summer Werner also received notice that he was to report for military training. Any young man, unless essential to a particular field of industry or research, could be called up to serve in the *Wehrmacht* or Luftwaffe. Refusal to do so would almost certainly lead to arrest and imprisonment, or worse. Kitka recalled the day that dreaded letter arrived at Werner's parents' home.

> It was very blunt; more or less a demand. There could be no argument; he would have to report to the local military authority firstly for a medical assessment. If medically fit then he would begin army training. My heart sank into my stomach from this news. I was terrified that if Werner left to join the fighting I would never see him again. We had all taken to living down in the large cellar beneath the house. We had taken everything we needed down there, including beds, chairs, medical supplies and what food we had available. It was far too dangerous at this point to remain above ground with the aerial bombings intensifying daily. They were hitting the factories day and night. Stray bombs often fell near to Werner's parents' home.
>
> There was a rumour that Friedrichshafen would have to be turned into a fortress, which its people would have to defend from the invasion force coming from the west. Werner even discussed us running away from Friedrichshafen, but where would we go and how would we survive? It was

quite insane. He suggested we head west and hopefully we might be captured by the British, French or Americans. We would become refugees and our war would be over. I told him that was crazy and if we were caught we would almost certainly be brought back to Friedrichshafen and he would face a military court, where he might be shot for desertion. Then there was the question of how the children would cope on such a journey. We were both so scared of what might happen. We suggested all kinds of silly ideas. That evening down in the cellar I managed to get the children settled while Werner discussed things with his father. I lay awake listening to them talk into the early hours, then I drifted off to sleep, despite bombs landing close by during a night raid.

In the morning Werner took my hand and told me, "We are getting out of here and going to Switzerland." I looked at him as if he had gone mad. I said to him, "How the hell do you think we are going to get there? We will never make it." Werner looked into my eyes and said, "This is the beauty of corruption." Again, I asked what he was going on about. His father then intervened and told me that he had offered a substantial bribe to people he knew in high places; people he could trust who could help us. The Swiss border was not that far away and he promised that everything would be arranged for us to get out and remain in Switzerland until the outcome of the war had been decided. Again I questioned him about how we would support ourselves and guarantee the safety of the little ones. Switzerland was indeed neutral, but even if we made it there it would be doubtful whether we would be permitted to work or given any help. Werner's father intervened, "Everything will be taken care of. All you have to do is listen to me and do exactly as you are told. Now, can you do this or not?" I reluctantly agreed, but only because I was so scared of Werner going off to fight and not coming back. We were totally and utterly in love and wanted to marry and live the rest of our lives together. There were so many complications to consider. I could not tell little Roel's father what we planned to do as I was fearful he would inform on us out of spite. I knew he was still very much in love with me but I just felt I could not trust him with something like this. He was insanely jealous of Werner and often threatened that if the war came to Friedrichshafen he would shoot Werner dead in revenge for stealing his wife. Werner's father had several meetings with people over the weeks that followed. I know that very little money was exchanged but items of gold and jewellery were. In fact, a lot of gold was handed over by Werner's father and mother as payment. Werner's father explained, "German money would have little value in the event that Germany loses this war. Gold is the currency of corruption and everyone takes it. It can be hidden and used after the war when all of this is over." It was pretty obvious we were losing the war. Rats everywhere were preparing to leave the sinking ship of National Socialism. All of them, particularly those in local government, were looking for nest eggs. They themselves would soon be fleeing in the hope of starting new lives after the war. For the next few weeks we discussed the plan for getting out and going to Switzerland. We were sworn to secrecy to tell no one at all.

Just a week before everything was in place [...] our world came crashing down around us. We were in the cellar when we heard heavy boots outside. The front door of the house was smashed in and the heavy boots came clattering down into the cellar. Guns were pointed at us and we were told we were all under arrest. Werner's aunt had to take Roel and Alice while we were taken away for questioning. We were taken firstly to a little police station. We were there for just a few hours when these men arrived. The black leather coats and hats were ones we were only too familiar with. These were Gestapo; the dreaded Nazi secret police. We were told to go outside and were bundled into the back of a truck. Two of the men jumped in with us and one sat with his pistol in his hand. I knew we were in very serious trouble now and was terrified. We had no excuses; we had been caught red handed. We were being taken to the Gestapo headquarters in Berlin, we were told. I knew that was a long journey of many hours.

The truck stopped and pulled over off a road, which must have only been an hour or so into the journey. The two men in the back of the truck jumped out, and the driver and his passenger had also jumped out and were waiting for us. There were trees all around in a heavily wooded area. We were ordered to walk into the woods away from the road. We weren't stupid. We knew what this meant for us. To my horror they told me, "If you have anything to say to this man then you had better do it now and be quick." They were referring to Werner. All I could do was cry as I held him in my arms for the last time. I told him I loved him and he told me to be strong and that he loved me too. They dragged him a few yards away, placed a pistol to the base of his head and squeezed the trigger. I couldn't look. I covered my face with my hands as I heard the crack of the pistol. Then they grabbed Werner's father and asked him the same question. Werner's mother went hysterical and I had to hold her back. I tried to cover her eyes as a pistol was placed to the back of Werner's father's head and followed again that dreadful sound of someone being shot. I recall breaking down again and being on the ground. I thought they were going to shoot us now; both me and Werner's mother would be put against a tree and shot. We would be buried here and no one would ever know what had happened. Instead, they shouted at us to get back into the truck. The truck headed not for Berlin but back in the direction of Friedrichshafen. When we arrived back at the police cells it was dark. I was told that my two children would be handed over to the care of my former spouse, Joachim Obermann. I felt as if I was dying inside and wished that I had never allowed Werner or his father to have even considered this stupid plan. So many visions tormented my mind as I lay in the cell that night. Several times in the night I heard the viewing port in the cell door open. Someone was looking in on me.

I had lost all touch of time but it must have been the next day when they came into my cell; a room with the windows blocked out with black paint or something similar. One of them dragged a table into the room and I wondered what this was for. It did not take long to find out what they were going to do with me. Four of them came in and one ordered me to remove my clothes. I asked them why and for my trouble I received a heavy slap to the side of my face. I removed my clothing and two of them grabbed me and held me down on the table. I knew what they were going to do with me and gritted my teeth and shut my eyes. Each one took his turn with me. Before each rape they put on birth control and called me a whore, dog, bitch and other obscenities. When they had finished playing with me my clothes were taken away and I was thrown these dirty pair of trousers and a plain grey jacket. They told me I would be joining other non-conformers for work duty in the next few days. They wouldn't tell me what work I would be doing, or for how long, but I guessed it would not be pleasant.

The work that Kitka Obermann was assigned to was the living nightmare of joining concentration camp prisoners from Dachau and Dora-Mittelbau. Kitka was forced to join hundreds of slave labourers, mainly from the east, to assist with the construction of tunnels outside the city of Friedrichshafen. Kitka recalled her time there:

It was a living hell. No other word can describe it. I was classed as a non-conformist and a traitor and had I been a man I would have been shot, as Werner and his father had been. I often wished they would just shoot me too. From early morning until very late at night, sometimes into the early hours, I had to join a queue which passed heavy buckets of soil and stones to one of the tunnel entrances. We had SS in place as guards and they would beat you if they felt you were not working hard enough. The labourers were mostly men who could not speak German. They looked at me, puzzled, wondering what I was doing here or what I had done to be here. The guards changed shifts and one of them, a young man whose name I can no longer recall, took pity on me. He asked me how I came to be here and what offence I had committed against the Reich. I told him, but we were often interrupted by other guards. So they did not suspect anything he would pretend to shout at me and kick me. When the other guards moved on up the line into the darkness he would apologise and continue talking to me. It was odd. He would scream and beat up the other labourers but would show me compassion and even brought me food and water. That young man helped me to survive but condemned others to their deaths. He would tell me, "You are much too beautiful to be in this place." He would talk about the war and how the new V-weapons, as they were called, would change the face of warfare and that at least I was helping in that respect. He would say that maybe after the war I might receive a pardon if I had learned my lesson and that maybe he could take me for dinner. It was just so surreal. I often cried my heart out thinking about Werner while I worked. His face was in my head all of the time, and my children too. I wondered what had become of them, if they were safe and if I would ever see them again. Over the weeks that followed my weight plummeted. I would look at my arms and think they looked like that of a corpse. They had shaved off my hair to help prevent lice, but lice still infested your clothing due to the insanitary conditions of the camp. I lost all notion of day and night as we worked in darkness and emerged in the darkness. After four hours sleep we would trudge back into those tunnels in the dark.

I don't know how long it was, maybe a month, maybe two months, when I was called out of the work party. They used a fire hose and washed me down like some kind of animal. I was given some clean clothing and I asked them, "Why are you doing this?" It was Joachim who had discovered everything that had happened and had been desperately petitioning for my release, stating that I had probably been brainwashed by the Bothe family. This, of course, was not the case, but it was probably the only thing he could think of. I was held in a cell and given slightly better food, and even a small cup of black coffee, which was something I hadn't drunk in a very long time. I was very confused and in a kind of delirium. I was told to sign several forms. I don't even remember what they were for or what they said. After some days I was told a visitor had come to see me. Through the door walked Joachim Obermann, who instantly broke down and sobbed as he saw the state I was in. He embraced me and sobbed like a lost child. When he recovered his composure he explained that he could sign papers and I would be permitted to return home, but only into his care and me as his wife. I just nodded to him and he left the room, returning some minutes later having signed some paperwork.

To this day I don't know what exactly he did or how he did it, but he got me out of there. Maybe corruption played a part. I am not sure. All that I remember is that we left that dreaded place and I slept most of the journey to the house that me and Joachim had once shared together. When we arrived the children were asleep in their beds. I was able to have a look at them briefly then Joachim made me a bed in the spare room. I stayed there for the next few weeks as I felt so ill and every part of my body hurt. It was some days after returning home that Joachim sat at the end of the bed and told me, "You know I will always love you, Katherine, despite all that has happened. I take no joy in what happened to the Bothes, even though I was angry at the time. Had I looked after you better and maybe treated you more as a wife all of this would not have happened. If you still wish to leave when all of this is over, I will not stop you, and you have my word on that." He remarked at how much Alice looked like me and that he and his family had treated her with as much love as was given to Roel. The baby had grown and I felt I had already missed out so much. We spent so much time in the cellar of the house. It was nauseating as the darkness brought on panic attacks from the time I had spent in the tunnels. I had begun to have nightmares in my sleep too. I suffered from bouts of depression and all I wanted to talk about was Werner and his family but I felt I couldn't do this after all Joachim and his family had done to get me out of the mess I had ended up in.

Like many women in Germany at the time, I was not alone in this situation. It also made me question the whole morality of the Nazi Party and our Führer, Adolf Hitler.

What kind of world would we be living in if he succeeded in winning this war? I had become one of those tortured souls from the east. I had experienced the same violence, brutality and contempt many Germans had for them. I had changed within myself and began to think differently. Nazism was something that could not succeed in the world. It was evil in every single respect. I also understood that Nazism, however much it had once benefited my own existence, had to be destroyed. The thing was, how many Germans would have to die before they realised this? It was obvious Hitler was not winning the war. It was just a matter of time from the whispers we would hear. I promised that, if I survived this, I would change. For the time being I would just survive. It was all about survival as 1944 drew to a close. I remember my mother and father visiting me after three months. They were their normal repugnant selves, berating me for being stupid and behaving like a common slut and saying, "Maybe this time you have learned your lesson." They were far from sympathetic, but I understood that I was undeserving of sympathy. I also felt that we had no sympathy for the Jews who had disappeared from our society, or the slave workers taken from their homes in the east and brought here to be worked to death. It was during a conversation when I tried my best to not get angry that the question of where Werner Bothe and his father had been buried. My father laughed and snapped, "Graves you ask for? Traitors have no grave!"

Gertrud Koerg, along with her two younger sisters, was still living with her grandparents near their home city of Kassel. Their mother, Helena, who was also living with them, had bad days and good days considering the bereavement the family had experienced. The centre of Kassel was virtually uninhabitable by late 1944. The lack of food supplies and onset of winter, combined with the realisation that all was going very badly for Germany, exacerbated an already intolerable lifestyle on the German home front. Gertrud recalls:

Kassel had been very heavily bombed in the October of the previous year. That attack over two days last October broke the back of the city and its people. Many fled and never went back to their homes. Everything was almost completely destroyed over those two days and ten thousand recorded as being killed. Many of the friends I had known from the BDM had gone. Their parents had decided enough was enough and they just left their homes. I lost six of my closest friends to the bombing attacks. There were not many of us left now. My grandparent's home was about twenty-three miles from the city centre. Bombs fell near the house many occasions. We heard the bombs at night as the bombers jettisoned their loads for various reasons. Some had been hit by flak and dropped their bombs anywhere and turned back. They didn't care if their bombs landed on civilian areas or not. We were woken up by the explosions some nights. Next morning I would go with friends from the BDM and local boys to look for shrapnel in the bomb craters. There were some pieces of shrapnel that were just too heavy for me to carry home. The boys filled their backpacks with pieces of bombs, and some of them had very big collections of bomb and flak shrapnel. What they did with these after the war is anyone's guess. Our grandmother hated me bringing home shrapnel […]. She wouldn't let me bring it into her house and so it stayed outside in the woodshed. There was no school at this time and my mother, when she felt well enough, would teach us things herself, along with our grandmother. My grandmother had many old books from the pre-Nazi era on Germanic history, geography and maths and things. Our mother was still very much distraught at the loss of our father. If I cried I did so away from everyone. I had to be the strong one now and help look after us all. Our role as BDM girls had prepared us for struggle, pain and hardship. A woman's life is always struggle and hardship and that will never change, will it?

Ilsa Koerg also recalls what she terms today as the 'writhing corpse of National Socialism' in late 1944:

It was freezing cold. Sometimes we had no fire and if there was no fire we couldn't cook anything. Have you ever tried eating a raw potato? It's quite disgusting, but sometimes that's all we had to eat. I know Gertrud used to go out with her friends looking for anything we could burn on the fire or eat. I wanted to go with them but our grandparents and our mother would always say, "No, you have to stay here. It is not safe for you out there." I used to get very bored, stuck inside the house all day. Hunger would make you pace around like an angry cat.

Helga Koerg, the youngest, also recalls:

I remember still being excited when it snowed that winter. I would be allowed out a short while to play in the snow. Our mother worried constantly about us not eating properly and catching some illness. She was convinced that she would lose us all. After our father had died she changed so much. She became so thin, sad and withdrawn. I recall her spending hours staring out the window. She did this a lot. Our grandparents tried to distract her from her sadness but she seemed trapped within her own dark world.

I remember some Luftwaffe soldiers arriving one morning in the snow. They came and knocked on the door and they talked with grandfather for a few minutes before leaving. They came back an hour later with some wood, root vegetables and some pork. Apparently they had shot a pig and wanted to eat it. They were welcomed in and helped prepare some of the meat for a stew, which was soon boiling away after a fire was lit with the logs they had supplied. They asked us our names and they gave us some of their sweet rations. My mother sat in the living room looking out of the window, as she used to do much of the time. One of them said hello to her through the doorway. I recall my mother looking at him and smiling, then looking away again. It was grandmother who explained what had happened to our father. The Luftwaffe boys sat and listened intently and I'm pretty sure I saw a tear roll down the cheek of one of them. He wiped it away with the sleeve of his heavy, grey coat. Then he began to talk about the war in the east and that going there was every German soldier's worst nightmare. My grandparents questioned them about the progress of the war in the Russia and if they felt we could push the Russians back. I remember one replying, "God help us if they ever get here. They are an enemy unlike any other; savage and hell-bent on vengeance. They attack in waves. You can kill one, two, three, four thousand of them and more will keep coming behind." One of the Luftwaffe boys then commented that we would crush them with our new V-2 weapons. I remember asking them what a V-2 was. They explained it was a kind of bomb that could travel far across seas and continents and land in the enemy heartland with great destructive power, that nothing could stop it and they would have no warning of it coming. One of them even drew a pencil sketch of what it looked like. I still have that sketch today as I kept it inside one of my story books.

We were grateful for those flak boys visiting. The meat and vegetables they had given us made a stew which warmed our bodies and made us feel happier. We had wood for the fire for a few days, but would use it only on colder days. We all slept downstairs together. Me, Ilsa and Gertrud would be in the middle while our grandparents and mother were on the outside. We used each other's body heat to keep warm and slept with our hats, gloves and winter boots and coats on. Even then it was still bitterly cold sometimes. The Christmas of that year was nothing to celebrate really. Unlike the Christmases we had shared years ago, we had nothing. We had our lives, of course, but that Christmas morning of 1944 I sat in the cold and thought of father, and I just cried. Then Ilsa began to cry, and before I knew it everyone but Gertrud was crying. Gertrud was the one who was always trying to comfort us, cheer us all up, and keep us all strong. I don't know how she was able to do it and cope herself. All I can say is that it made us incredibly close all our lives. Gertrud once told us, "If it means having to die to protect you, then I would die." The thing was, she actually meant it and she was so very young herself. Just a young teenage girl having to be strong for all the madness and sorrow this war had brought about.

I remember our earliest school days, how we were taught that Jews were these vile beasts, that they were responsible for our misery and the war. That Jews controlled the wealth of the world for their own ends and wanted Germany destroyed. We would be told that the cattle trucks leaving for Auschwitz were doing so with our nation's preservation in mind. I began to reflect upon all these things. When I was alone I would begin to think about it. Even though I was very young I felt a tinge of sadness, that somehow all of this was wrong. Gertrud would warn me never to say anything. She would say, "You don't say anything against the Führer. It is one of the most dangerous things you can do." She was just warning us about people hearing us complain as some would report you to the authorities, even if you were friends. […] The fear of treachery was everywhere now. Whole families could be accused of being traitors. Those presumed guilty in puppet courts were often taken away into the forest and shot, and buried in an unmarked grave. There were rumours of people being taken into the forest by the SS, Gestapo or SRD and shot and buried there. These rumours became far too prevalent to have been fictitious. It became a bit of a saying amongst those feeling dissent that "traitors have no grave". Better to conform than lie dead in unconsecrated soil.

Chapter 13

A Little Town Called Seelow

The little town of Seelow lies in the province of Brandenburg (Prussia) and was a typically sleepy German town before the Second World War arrived with all its fury. As German forces were pushed back from the east by the advance of the Red Army, this insignificant little town would become one of a number of strategically valuable objectives for the Red Army. The Battle of the Seelow Heights would go down in history as one of the most savage of the Second World War. For Germany, the outcome of the battle was critical. Close to one million Soviet soldiers of the 1st Belorussian Front (including 78,556 soldiers of the Polish 1st Army) were advancing on Berlin. If the German defenders at Seelow failed in their objective to defend the high ground, then the gates to the German capital would be prised open. Over the weeks prior to the battle reinforcements were sent to Seelow. Many of these were boys – and girls – of the Hitler Youth, along with members of the people's militia, or *Volkssturm*.

Sixteen-year-old Maria Goetze and her mother, Stephanie, were in Sachsendorf, near Seelow, prior to and during the battle. They experienced first-hand the savagery of war in what had been an idyllic little town. Maria recalled:

> By this time in 1944 there could be no ignorance whatsoever could there? You would have had to have been stupid to believe all of the propaganda that the Nazis were now spouting off. The first sign for us personally was the rationing of food and everyday essentials. I think this started in late 1943 and we were soon issued with these paper tokens for bread and things. It was barely enough to live on for me and my mother. My father was a soldier and he was fighting in the west somewhere. By the middle of 1944 we had received no mail from father and were extremely worried about him.

In Sachsendorf we were a small community who looked after one another. It was an emergency situation and we had to get together to help one another survive. Of course, people were doing what we did in every town, village and city in Germany at the time. In our community we had midwives, doctors, butchers and bakers. We had all we needed until late 1944, when all available men were rounded up and ordered to report for military service under emergency regulations. I remember my mother and I were out in the street once when these very young men from the SRD [*Streifendienst*], the Hitler Youth police, began to round up men of all ages and gather them together. One SRD shouted "You are all fit, are you not? You are all able to walk and hold a weapon. You are all able and therefore required by the Führer's decree to defend the Reich from our enemies. Unless you wish to become the slaves and dogs of Bolsheviks you will fight any way you can." One old man interrupted saying, "We don't want to fight. We are better here looking after our wives and the children." A scuffle broke out, and before my mother could even cover up my eyes an SRD had pushed this man up against a wall, pushed a pistol into his throat and pulled the trigger. The man's lifeless body slumped to the ground and there was a large bloody stain left on the wall. Curious children looked at it afterwards when the SRD left and there were pieces of brain tissue stuck to the stone. My mother said "It's all breaking down now." She took my hand and we went home.

One day I was outside in our garden when I heard rumbles in the distance. I thought maybe a storm was on its way. It sounded like distant thunder but hours later the sound was still there. I was playing with my skipping rope when an engine roared overhead. I dropped my skipping rope and climbed up onto the wall to see what it was. I stood gazing up into the sky and watched this aeroplane rolling and climbing. It made several circuits of the village and I watched it closely. On the last circuit I watched it dive down very low. It flew straight and level for a few seconds then there was this very loud crack of gunfire. I could clearly see the fire coming from the aeroplane's wings. My mother had by this time jumped up and grabbed me, screaming for me to get inside the house. Before we got to the back door I saw the aeroplane and the big red stars on the underside of its wings. It was a Russian attack plane; the first Russian aircraft I had ever seen. A few days later some of the local boys had picked up these large brass bullet casings from the Russian plane. They guarded these trophies as prized possessions. One of them was my friend, Berthold, and he was very excited. I remember holding them in my hands and thinking what damage something like this would do if it hit you or your house. I was not allowed outside much after that. We had a shelter below ground out in the garden. It had been there since the First World War and had been built by an elderly former resident who, they say, spent more hours in there than in his house […].

I recall the reinforcements pouring through on their way to the high ground to the east; hundreds and hundreds of them, with artillery, anti-tank weapons and anti-aircraft guns. I saw vehicles carrying huge rolls of vicious-looking barbed wire. Our soldiers marched wearily past on their way to the high ground, where we had been told they were digging trenches, ready to fight. There were bunkers and trenches being dug around Sachsendorf. The SRD even visited our house and told my mother and me, "You should prepare yourselves for the coming battle." They left us each a *Panzerfaust* [single-shot anti-tank weapon] on our doorstep along with this sheet of paper on how it should be used. The *Panzerfaust* was a weapon designed for anyone to be able to use. It was deadly against most tanks but you had to use it at close range. I remember my mother saying to me, "Maria, you leave those things alone. You are not to touch them under any circumstances." When it was dark later I saw my mother take the two *Panzerfausts* and throw them into a hedge a short distance away from our house. Mother was of the opinion that we should have no one's blood upon our hands.

As the soldiers dug in around us we found it easier to find things to eat. I remember there used to be this flour mill near our home. We went up there to see what we could find and when we got there, we discovered it had been taken over by our soldiers. I saw the barrels of machine guns poking out from the open windows. My mother began talking with the soldiers and they gave her some of the last remaining flour and some bread rolls which the soldiers had made themselves. We were so excited that we had some bread. A thing so many of you take for granted today was like gold back then. One of the soldiers said to me, "Hello, little hamster girl. Here, you can have these." He gave me some sweets from his own rations. They used to call you a hamster if you went out scavenging. That's why he called me "little hamster girl". My mother talked with the soldiers for almost an hour. She was telling them about father, who was fighting in the west. The soldiers reassured her that if he was a prisoner of war he would be better off in British or American hands than the Soviets. The last thing they said to her was, "You really need to get away from here. Take your child and leave if you have any sense." Mother then told them about the SRD who had been coming round. One of the young German soldiers said, "Ah yes, little boy soldiers with too much power. Their turn will come though."

We returned home with quite a little haul of goodies. Though we would have to make them last as long as we could. On the way home through the woods there was that distant sound again, like thunder rolling across the heavens on a stormy night. Only the skies were clear there was no thunder or rain. The next day more Russian planes were over our area. I said to mother, "Where is the Luftwaffe?" Most of the day was spent inside. Christmas Day 1944 was sad and cold. I wrapped myself in my blankets and could not help but think of sweetmeats, roast potatoes, pork, cakes and the joys we had experienced as a family, which now felt so long ago. Some fantastic news was passed to us later in the day. Father had been captured by the British and was now a prisoner of war. The document passed to us explained he was well. This in a sense was the best Christmas gift we could ever have hoped for. All we had to do was survive this war and maybe we would be reunited someday.

Maria's mother never spoke of her experiences of the Second World War with anyone. She found much of what she had witnessed too horrific to convey to even her closest family and friends. Stephanie Goetze did, however, keep a personal journal. She had always found it easier to write words down in her journal than have to relive them with the words from her own mouth. Maria very kindly sent me the translated extracts which were relevant to the Seelow battle.

> There had been a steady build-up of our forces in the area. Tanks, artillery and thousands of our soldiers had passed through our village. They were well dug in on the higher ground in anticipation of an enemy attack. The soldiers who stopped and spoke with us all told us we should evacuate to Berlin as soon as possible, and that it would be too dangerous for me and my child to remain here. I told them we would not run anywhere; we wanted to stay in our home. In the end though we were called on by a neighbour, who insisted we should join them and others in a farmhouse to the north-west of the village. I reluctantly told Maria to pack a small bag with some clothes, get a coat and blanket and then we left to go with the others to the farmhouse.
>
> When we arrived at the farm we were greeted by the others there, including some people we knew quite well. The farm had an extensive cellar which was located beneath a barn and away from the main house itself. The cellar had been stocked with so many provisions. Both me and Maria were shocked to see cheese, potatoes, preserved jams and vegetables, and smoked meat, which hung from hooks on one of the beams that ran across the ceiling. There were two large oil lamps down there and a pile of candles, along with buckets of water for toilet use and washing. There was a deep, cosy mattress of straw for sleeping on. The cellar was a little chilly and you could

see the steam from your mouth as you breathed. It was quite deep underground and we all felt quite safe once we were settled.

We knew that a battle was imminent. Something in the air just made you feel that something was going to happen. We rarely ventured out of the cellar, and if we did we did not go very far. On 15 April we were down in the cellar, talking about things. It was more nervous chatter than actual coherent conversation. We were all very frightened and I held Maria close to me at all times. Earlier in the day we heard a lot of air activity, but could not tell whose aircraft they were, theirs or ours. We had not seen a Luftwaffe aircraft for weeks now so assumed they were enemy reconnaissance planes. They flew low over the area, carrying out several circuits before flying off.

That night was relatively still. Maria read one of her books by the light of the oil lamp while we adults talked about things. I told Maria to put her book away and that we should get some sleep. We went and lay down in the straw with the blanket over us and soon the conversation of the others was lost in blissful slumber. It was around 3am, or maybe just after – I don't remember fully what the time was – when there was this terrible noise. I awoke with a start, my heart pounding in my chest and a feeling of nausea due to the pitch blackness of the cellar. Herr Riedel was startled by the noise too and immediately lit one of the oil lamps, but kept it on a low setting so as not to disturb the others. The noise above grew in intensity. The explosions sounded like thunder rolling across the ground above us. It was the worst noise I had heard in the entire war and it went on and on. Maria woke suddenly in a panic and began shouting "Mummy! Mummy!" I quickly went to her and comforted her. She was crying through fear. I told her, "It will be alright, sweet child." The ground shook from the intensity of the explosions above and the others began to question if it was safe to stay here. Would the cellar collapse under the bombardment? Herr Riedel assured us all that nothing other than a direct hit from a heavy bomb would bring this cellar down on us. There was a building above and it was hoped that if it was hit this would take most of the force. There was a small tunnel that we could use as an emergency exit, but Herr Riedel explained he had not used this tunnel for two years so didn't know what its condition might be.

There were lulls in the bombardments and Herr Riedel was of the opinion this was to allow enemy forces to advance. When there were lulls we would quickly go up above ground to see what was happening. Some of our soldiers came to the farm and said they would need to commandeer one of the outbuildings so they could use it to treat their wounded. One of the soldiers asked if there were women here. Herr Riedel asked them why. He was told, "We need women to comfort the wounded. Women are better at this than men." Herr Riedel came and told us about the situation, but he was reluctant that any of us become involved or exposed to any of the dangers. I told him I would help but that Maria must stay in the cellar and not be left alone. Herr Riedel gave me his assurances, so I agreed to help in the first-aid station. We prepared buckets of clean water and the soldiers brought bandages and disinfecting fluid. The wounded men were brought in from the heights. Some of the injuries were horrific and I knew that these badly injured men were not going to survive to see their families again. They came in with arms and legs blown off. Some came in with an arm or leg hanging on by a thread of skin. There were shrapnel wounds, gunshot wounds and wounds caused by rockets and bombs. A number of Katyusha rockets had landed in our neighbourhood. The exploded metal tubes peeled back like mushrooms, sending large steel shards over a wide area. There was shrapnel embedded in the walls of the farmhouse and outbuildings. I spent a few hours each day helping the other women to make wounded men more comfortable. Many were then evacuated to Berlin. We could only have so many of them here before it was too full. The worst cases were left to die while those who could be saved and the less badly injured were treated. It was such a harsh and terrible thing to have to do, to prioritise who would live and who would die, but that was how it was. The fighting soon appeared to overtake us. The last of the injured were taken and then the soldiers told us, "The doors to Berlin had been broken open. We are falling back now for the last battle." We were told to leave and go with them as the Soviets were now approaching with great speed, but we told them we did not want to leave our homes. One of the soldiers left me with a chilling thought when he said, "For God's sake, get out of here. You have no idea of what they will do to you […]". I suppressed these thoughts as I went back down into the cellar with the others. There was nothing we could do now apart from wait it out. We knew the war was lost and it was no longer a big deal. The deal now was survival; that was the goal.

I recall the day the Russians did arrive. We heard them above ground, moving around the buildings searching for any signs of life or hidden enemy. They shouted out in Russian and we cowered down in the cellar like scared rabbits. None of us dared make a sound. You could hear a pin drop in the dark silence. Then we heard the sound of boots walking around above us and the sound of voices. There was a scratching sound coming from the entrance to the cellar. A chink of light appeared as the heavy oak door was forced open. Then a voice barked out in broken German, "Anyone in there come out now or we will throw in grenades." Herr Riedel shouted, "There is no cause for grenades. There are just women and children and an old man down here. We are surrendering to you." One by one we stood up and walked up the ladder and out through the exit into the barn outside. There was no violence or abuse, but we were searched and the cellar was searched too for weapons or any German soldiers we might have been hiding. They found only the corpses of those who had died in the aid post. They even searched these bodies, taking rings, paperwork, money and anything else they fancied. The German-speaking Russian asked me, "Is this your girl?" pointing to Maria. I told him, "Yes, she is mine, and she is all I have left now." He then asked me, "Where is your man? Where are all the men from this place?" I told him my husband was a prisoner of war in the west and that the other men from here were taken by the SRD months ago and were threatened at gunpoint. He seemed to be happy with my explanation and then began giving orders to his men. We were asked which direction the German soldiers went when they left and we had to show them on a map.

Over the next few days they seemed to filter out, heading towards Berlin. As they moved out they just stared at us and said nothing. There were no facial expressions to gauge their emotions or anything. As they moved off other Russians came, but these were different. These Russian soldiers were abusive and we quickly decided to go back into the cellar, shut the door and hope they would leave us all alone. For the first night they left us alone but the next morning they opened the cellar and came down. They took our lamps and the small amount of food that was left. One of them spat at us and muttered something. Herr Riedel, who was stood beside me, pushed Maria behind him out of sight. The Russians then left us alone. We knew if more came they would look down here and bother us. Herr Riedel insisted that Maria hide beneath the straw when the Russians came. I had no reason to feel threatened. So far the worst that had been done to us was to be spat upon.

A week later yet more Soviets passed through our village while others decided to camp up near the farm. One of them came and told us, "Hitler is dead. Germany has lost the war. The war is over." Me and Maria just wanted to go home to our house to see if it was still standing. Against the better judgement of Herr Riedel, we walked out through a small wood that we used as a short cut to get to our house. As we walked through the woods if felt good to be out in the fresh air instead of being shut up in the cellar. We could see the faint light of a campfire but we ignored it and hurried on through the wood. We could also hear Russian voices and hoped they would take no notice of us. As we neared the clearing, which brought us out to the roadway that led to our house, we saw a gang of Russian soldiers standing around. One was drinking from a bottle. They were just stood there talking until we approached. They stopped and looked at us and then blocked our path. This was the most frightened I had ever been in my life. They were touching our hair and talking to each other, but we could not understand what was being said. I thought that they were going to do something to us but they just searched our pockets and then let us go.

As we hurried away along the road we passed many houses that were just flattened rubble. There was no one else around. We rounded the corner and there was our little house, still standing but with a very large hole in the one wall. We peered through the hole and saw that the kitchen was destroyed completely. Every room inside the house had been looted and my parent's china smashed to pieces. This upset me more than anything as it was sentimental. We knew we couldn't stay there and so picked up a few things and headed back to the farm. We did not want to go through the woods this time as our earlier experience had frightened us. We decided to go the road way, which took longer but we felt would be safer. As we trudged silently back along the road to the farm we heard a truck coming up behind us. We thought it would just pass by but it pulled over a few hundred yards up the road ahead of us. There were five Russians in the truck; two in the front and three in the back. The three in the back asked us where we were going. I told them and they then told us to get in the back as they were going that way. I declined their offer and said "thanks", and was about to walk away when the one in the passenger seat said, "Hey, we were not asking you, woman, we were telling you. Now get in the fucking back." I thought about running as there were trees all around and we might run and hide. I knew if we could make the 200yds or so to the trees we could disappear into the woods and hide. I looked at the man in the passenger seat and I said, "Okay, thank you, we will come with you." I grasped Maria's hand tightly as I could without hurting her and we walked to the rear of the truck. Just as one of them put his hand down to pull us up into the back I screamed "run!" Holding Maria's hand, I ran and pulled her with me, though she soon overtook me as we ran for our lives. I told her to head for the trees to the right and to keep running fast as she could. We crashed through bushes which cut our arms and faces. Yet we kept running, petrified that the Russians were behind us. We ran until we were in agony and couldn't run any more. We lay on the ground, exhausted, our hearts pounding in our chests. We lay there looking all around us, but were alone. The Russians had probably driven off after we had run off. I did not ever wish to be in that situation again. Had they got us in that truck we would have almost certainly been raped.

We made it back to the farm just as it was getting dark. Herr Riedel went mad when we told him what had happened. He cursed me for putting young Maria in danger and told us we were to stay here now until some form of order was restored. We did as Herr Riedel told us. Later we went to Berlin [...] as I wanted to try and find my husband. It took nearly seven months before we were all reunited. I wanted us to all go back home, but my husband insisted we remain in the areas under control of the western Allied authority. I asked him why we couldn't go back and he just said, "We need to stay away from the Russian-controlled sectors. Please trust me on this, Stephanie."

Maria and her parents settled in West Germany. They spent four years on a farm before moving into a home they could once again call their own. They had made it through the war alive. Maria reflects on this:

Yes, we made it through it all. Yet the poison of Nazism had to be drained from the veins of German society, particularly the young people like myself. We had to admit that we had all made mistakes, both young and old. The mistakes we had made as a people and a society had cost over six million people their lives. Are we really all that different from one another? When people ask me ""Where were you in the war? What did you do." I tell them, "I came from a little town called Seelow, and what did I do? Well, that is easy. I survived".

Chapter 14

Exequy

'The war is over, you're still alive, you think you're safe, but it's all lies.'

The death of Nazi Germany in May of 1945 was not a pleasant sight to behold. With Hitler's suicide and the Soviet capture of Berlin, the Third Reich was finally at an end. There were no more shots being fired, no more bombs falling and no more home front. The struggles that lay ahead in peacetime Germany were, at times, just as severe as those experienced during the years of war. Many of Germany's cities lay in ruin; rail and transport networks destroyed. All of this was compounded by the influx of German refugees from the former German-held eastern territories as many of the Germans who had moved there had now been expelled. The Allies understood that Germany would need rebuilding. This would take many years to complete, even though a degree of urgency began to creep in following the deteriorating relations between east and west. There were many who felt that Germany should be left as one huge ruin and receive no help in reconstruction. As extreme an opinion as this was, we have to remember that many of the wounds were still open at this stage. As the Russians advanced toward Berlin they liberated many of the forced labour and death camps; places that would become infamous in world history. I have already written extensively in previous books on how the Red Army vented its anger upon the German population, so feel this needs no further explanation. In this final chapter I will explore the lives of those Germans who were outside the Soviet-occupied areas.

Alessa Goberg has some interesting recollections from the aftermath of the Second World War:

> The arrival of British and American forces in our zone was more or less expected by 1944. We could have abandoned the farm and fled, but where would we have run to and how

would we have lived? We would have just caused problems elsewhere by leaving everything behind and turning up on someone else's doorstep. It was not our way of doing things. We had seen our own troops retreating from the advance of the Western Allies. They were pursued with tanks, aircraft and artillery, and thousands of infantry. Their aircraft roared overhead at treetop height and would shoot at anything that moved. Even after the announcement that the war was over we felt it would be too risky to take a horse and cart out on the roads. The Allied air force was rightly very jumpy as there were still small pockets of resistance here and there.

When the Allied soldiers came they said very little. They made a thorough search of the whole farm. They wanted to know if we were hiding anyone or had any weapons hidden away. My father explained he had a gun which he needed for his own personal use, but there were no other weapons on the farm. The British soldier in charge politely asked to see my father's gun. So my father went and fetched it for him. The British man obviously knew his weapons as he checked my father's gun and remarked it was not even loaded. It was explained that the rifle was used mainly for deer and boar hunting and the controlling of pests on our farmland. After this the rifle was handed back to my father. My father went to return his gun to the house and caught soldiers looting and stuffing our possessions into their kit bags and pockets. My father threatened them with the rifle. There was some commotion so we ran inside to see what was going on. I went in through the door to see my father on the ground and these two gorillas standing over him. One was threatening him with a handgun. I pushed past them and stood between them and my father. I asked him, "Are you alright? Did they hurt you?" He said, "No, they didn't. They just pushed me over and began stealing our things." The officer came in and there were some heated words from him, judging by the tone of his voice. The three soldiers then emptied their bags and pockets of the things they had tried to steal. They went into the barn and tore it apart looking for anyone who might be hiding. We knew no one who would be hiding so we let them do it. It was explained to us in German that there were people the Allies were looking for. These people were responsible for war crimes and were now on the run. They turned all of the outbuildings upside down but found no weapons or war criminals hiding in the hay. It was all very stressful and some of our things did get stolen, even after what had happened in the house.

Once these lot moved on another lot would come and the same things would happen again and again. I wondered if they'd ever leave us alone to get on with our lives. The important thing now was to get any supplies of food we had out into the local villages and towns, where it could be used to feed our people. New crops had to be planted, and animal feed prepared for the winter. There was so much to do and barely anyone to help do it, and all the time we had soldiers demanding to search our home. Then they would steal your things if they had chance. It got better after a few months, but we knew hard times lay ahead, not just for us in the countryside but for everyone in Germany. To be honest, I was quite afraid of the future at that time. We were all under suspicion of being haters of Jews, and murderers and monsters who you could not trust. I know the British and Americans were issued with instructions that they should, under no circumstances, talk to us or accept any hospitality. This was an order issued by the Allied high command. It was impossible to enforce such a law and after some months had passed we were quite friendly with each other. I could not speak very much English, so it was difficult to talk to the Allied soldiers. They would try and gesture to you like, "Can I take a photo?" They would hold up their cameras and put their thumb up as if to say, "Is this okay?" It didn't bother me if they wanted to take photographs. Pretty soon I was having my photo taken with young British and American soldiers with their arms around me. Of course, some of them didn't like us at all. You would get cold stares and they would sometimes spit at you. But for the most part they behaved themselves. We didn't really hear much about Berlin until later on, when some German-speaking

American soldiers told us of what happened there. It all sounded too horrific to comprehend. I hoped it was all just propaganda. We soon knew it wasn't when we heard the stories from Germans who had escaped from the city. Some terrible things had happened in retaliation for us starting the war, and for our nation's behaviour during it. In one sense the home-front attitude continued as people did their best to survive. It would remain this way for a long time.

Roel Obermann had exhausted most of his mother's memoirs for inclusion in this book. Very few records remained from the immediate aftermath of the Second World War. Roel explains:

It was not a good time for my mother at all and that is something I recall vividly. She had gone back to live with my father and, for a short period, I know she tried hard to get back to a normal life with him. Even though I was young at the time I could see things were awkward between them. They had become more like roommates leading separate lives. I know they slept in the same bed but it was all an act. My younger stepsister, Alice, was only a baby so she knows nothing of that time. In the end I think, even though they both tried, all that they had been through proved too much.

My father had been an engineer for Dornier. He was questioned about the work he had been doing. The French, who were now occupying Friedrichshaffen, often called at our house and my father went off with them. He would return an hour or two later but would never reveal where he had been or what had been said. He would tell me, "You don't need to know, my boy." In the end my mother and father sat down and father said, "If a man captures a beautiful butterfly in his hands he cannot hold onto it forever. He has to let it go free." This was his way of saying goodbye and agreeing to a divorce. He did not need money he was in demand with his new French and American friends. He always wore a nice suit when he came to visit us, and he even left the house to us. That was a very honourable thing for him to have done and shows how much he still cared and loved our mother. [...] Our father spent a lot of time in America working on military aircraft projects. We did not see him that much until his retirement, when he returned to Germany. He never really spoke about his work, or the woman he had married and then divorced before he returned to Germany. As we grew older we noticed our mother had male friends who would take her out for dinner and things. She never committed to marriage again. I think she was always fearful of the past repeating itself.

As for the new French occupiers of our city, they had a harsh attitude towards us. If they even thought you had looked at them the wrong way in the street they would come over and belt you around the head. They were very vengeful to us Germans. I heard all kinds of stories of them taking women and assaulting them. I saw the looks they gave our mother when we went out. I remember us being followed by French soldiers of the occupying force. My mother became frightened and led us up an alleyway, pulled us over two garden walls and then ran with us until she felt sure the French soldiers were no longer following us. As some of the older people we knew used to say, "It is like Versailles all over again." We grew to understand what all this was about in school when we started. The Allied authorities were anxious that de-Nazification take place as soon as was possible. De-Nazification was forced down your throat, even if you had been too young to remember it. They wanted to make sure anyone with Nazi sympathies was erased from German society. One old man I knew said to me on this subject, "Good luck to them with it. They will need it." As our mother and father are now dead we can no longer ask them any questions. I think, had they been alive today, they would have both been reluctant to speak directly. My mother's writings are not an embarrassment to me at all. Maybe some day my son or daughter will inherit them, I don't know. The problem is that the youth today here in Germany really possess little interest in the darker aspects of our nation's history. It's all very sad really when you think about it.

The Koerg family were to witness four days of savage fighting when the battle for the city of Kassel began on 1 April 1945. The United States Third Army had advanced north-east from the Frankfurt region and the defence of Kassel fell to an infantry replacement battalion equipped with some heavy tanks, anti-aircraft guns and anti-tank weapons. The German attempt at defending Kassel was spirited, but doomed to fail. The *Wehrmacht* were already on the verge of collapse by the time the battle began. Many of the German soldiers preparing to face the Allied onslaught were men who were not only demoralised but also underequipped for the task facing them. The attacking Allied force was confident of a relatively quick victory over the defenders; they had superior numbers and firepower at their disposal.

Gertrud Koerg relates what happened as they prepared for what their grandfather referred to as a 'gathering storm':

> I remember the soldiers preparing their defences in the streets. They made barricades, dug trenches and set up positions in bombed-out buildings. There was a lot of movement in the fields and woods outside Kassel too. I remember the 8.8-cm anti-aircraft guns being brought forward, along with large boxes of ammunition. There were some Hitler Youth among the soldiers, but not many. The women, children and the old were hiding in the remains of their homes. Some were in bomb shelters in their gardens, in cellars beneath their homes or hiding in the countryside. When the battle began we had to stay below ground in our grandparents' cellar. The fighting started in the distance but you could tell from the noise that it was getting closer. For four days we stayed below ground while the fighting went on above us. We heard German voices in the house [...]. We could hear them running around and hear them shouting to one another, things like "Enemy a thousand yards to the west," then you would hear the blistering fire from machine guns. There was a lot of noise of weapons being fired then we could hear our soldiers steadily withdrawing into the centre of the city. It was quiet for a short time then we heard bullets hitting the outside walls of the house. They made a very distinctive sound as the

lead flattened against stone at supersonic speed. We knew the bullets could not penetrate the thick stone but we were worried they might use artillery and fire at the house we were hiding in. My mother, two sisters, grandpapa and grandmother all huddled together in the middle. We were frightened by what might happen next. Would the house come crashing in on us? It was the unknown that was the worst part about it all. We lost all sense of time as we never ventured out of the cellar.

The first we knew that American soldiers had arrived was the sound of a hand grenade exploding in one of the rooms above. They were clearing each room with explosives to ensure no one was waiting to ambush them. We heard them entering each room. Doors would be kicked down, there would be a loud bang, shots would be fired and people would enter the room. It was the usual routine that soldiers used to clear a building. We could make out American voices but we could not understand what was being said. The most frightening thing was that they might open the door to the cellar and throw a grenade down. We would have to alert them to the fact there were people down here. After a few minutes my mother began to call out *"Wir sind hier! Wir sind hier"* [we are here, we are here]. The cellar door was kicked with such force it was torn from its hinges and flew through the air, landing against the opposite wall of the cellar. Then a rifle muzzle menacingly came through the door. A voice in German bellowed down, "Come out and raise your hands!" The moment they saw us they calmed down as knew we were a family in hiding. When we had climbed out of the cellar they went in and searched it to make sure it was empty. Satisfied that it was empty, we were all searched for concealed weapons. I remember standing with my hands up as I was quickly searched, and the soldier then pulling my arms down again. The German-speaking one had his hands full as more people emerged from all over the place. They had captured, and injured, German soldiers, who were made to sit with their hands on their heads as if naughty children. We heard that the commander of the

German forces had offered his surrender. For us the war was now at an end. The Americans gave us all some water, which were desperate for. We had been sharing a bucket full of drinking water for the past few days and it had not been pleasant. We were told that we were now under the control of the American Allied military forces.

Ilsa Koerg recalls the fall of Kassel:

The American soldiers didn't seem that bad at all really. They were firm with us in many aspects, maybe even a little frosty at first. We were not offered sweets and things overnight. These things came about slowly. When they began to try and talk with us for example. I knew no language other than the German I grew up with. Yet we learned little pieces and sentences of English throughout the occupation, which was a good thing. I think in a way it showed them we were already changing because we were learning their language. We were all asked if we still thought Hitler was good, things like that. What could I say in answer to such questions? The Americans made sure we were told what our country had done with Europe's Jewish population. In time we were taken and shown the films of the death camps. The films showed a mountain of dead bodies, which was all the doing of our country. The films showed the men responsible and said that they would now be brought to justice. If you possessed anything with a Nazi symbol it was confiscated from you. The funny thing was that most of these things were then taken home by the Allied force as souvenirs. I know this because they told me so. It seemed they were fascinated by what our country had done. I was still only young and I could still have a childhood. Gertrud had done so much, and being older her time as a child had passed. Helga probably felt much the same way. I remember fondly the days when we all played together as children. By the time the war had ended we didn't do that anymore. We didn't play like children; we began to interact as adults.

Exequy

Helga Koerg agrees with her younger sister Ilsa:

> What Ilsa says is correct. Our childhood was over because
> of what we had been through. Our father's death still
> haunted us. That did not go away at all. Our mother still sat
> and stared from the windows, unable to carry on at times.
> I knew things were hard for her and she had a lot to deal
> with bringing us up. It was lucky we had the help of both
> sets of grandparents. We didn't want anyone to feel sorry
> for us. None of us wanted that at all. I know people who
> did go around crying for their lost sister, brother, mother
> or father, or other family. They were told, "Maybe now you
> will have some idea how the millions of Jewish families are
> feeling, knowing many of their family members are lying
> murdered in your country." It's true, of course. What our
> country did cannot be denied.

Helena Koerg's meticulous writings sadly ended as depression crushed
her spirit. As she grew older she talked less and less of her wartime
experiences as a wife on the German home front. At the mere mention
of her husband's name she would immediately become inconsolable
with grief. During the brief window of opportunity which did present
itself I had to be incredibly tactful. I was reminded about this on many
occasions by Gertrud, Helga and Ilsa, who were always at her side. Yet
there were moments where, for just a few minutes, the old woman's face
would become bright as she recalled amusing memories. Sadly, this time
was very brief. I cannot emphasise enough just how difficult this kind of
research can be.

The Koerg family had to change, like so many others in Germany.
The future at first appeared very bleak. Yet, due to the rapid political
changes that occurred, particularly for those in the east, they felt hopeful
of finding their own reconciliation with the rest of the world. As young
girls, Gertrud, Ilsa and Helga were very bright and did their mother proud
over the years that followed 1945. All were soon happily married with
careers and children of their own, and determined that their generation
would never repeat the mistakes made by their predecessors. Helena
Koerg died at the age of ninety-seven, with her beloved daughters and
grandchildren around her.

Ilsa Koerg spoke of her mother's passing in a positive sense, despite the grief:

> Our mother had started out in her life with everything she could have dreamt of. There were hardships, and when a certain individual came along and promised greater things for the German nation as a whole she and father believed it. I don't know how they personally felt about Jews as she never discussed these things with us. I don't think my parents were hateful people at all. They were naïve maybe, but certainly not hateful or violent. When our mother began to finally slip away from us we were all there with her. We all held her hand and said to her, "Dear mother, thank you for all you did for us. We will always love and cherish your memory and the time we had with you. Go to father now and take your love and ours to him." It was an extremely emotional time.

Adelaine Seidel, the young Berliner who lost her parents in an air raid on the city, recalled the final days of war in 1945:

> Those who were regarded as a biologically repugnant race of people were now all around us. Small groups of Germans sporadically managed to break through the Russian encirclement of Berlin, but these were very few. Once the city had been cut off that was it; anyone within that circle was trapped. We had many reports that the Russians were coming and were only twenty miles away from where we were. The noise of the battle going on in Berlin was tremendous. Lots of artillery fire was used, along with these things they called 'Stalin's Organ'. These were explosive rockets fired in salvos into the city to try and soften up any resistance.
>
> We were woken in the dawn mist one morning by someone shouting, "The Russians are here! The Russians are here!" It was a young woman and she ran about the camp repeating this over and over until everyone was aware of what was happening. We saw them [the Russians] in the distance,

approaching as a long, dark line. Soon the sounds of birds were drowned out by screeching tank tracks and mobile artillery guns. Our people were busy tearing up pieces of white cloth to make surrender flags. They tied the white material to the ends of sticks or twigs from the trees. There was the crack of a pistol and a group of us turned around to see that a wounded German soldier had shot himself through the left temple. His wife and child lay next to him. They were both lifeless and it looked like they had taken poison sometime during the night. I remember someone checking their bodies for signs of life and saying, "They are dead. There's nothing we can do." Terror seemed to run through everyone's body at the camp [Hitler Youth camp]. A number of the girls had their Hitler Youth jackets on and they took them off and threw them away. One desperately tried to burn her jacket on a small camp fire. The damp jacket just smouldered, refusing to burst into flame.

The Russian force sent their tanks in first to check us out, I guess. The tanks rolled up and soldiers came up behind them. We all walked forward, raising hands in the air so as not to cause any alarm. Some had their surrender flags, waving them above their heads. Their main focus of interest was the wounded soldiers with us. They went straight over to them and began searching them and asking them questions. One was dragged to his feet and struck a blow. We just clung to one another, hoping that things were not going to become ugly. I was with a girl older than me. Her name was Tia Wittmann and she had looked after me ever since I had arrived at the camp. The Russians knew from the number of young females present, and the uniforms and discarded items, that this was a Hitler Youth camp, which had been used as an evacuation post for children and other civilians. The Russians walked among us, picking things up and then throwing them aside. They tipped up small pots from their fires, checking to see what was in them. They grabbed pieces of bread and began eating it, only to spit it out after. They were not too worried about us and began to move on. They seemed eager to taste some action and get into Berlin. A few of their tanks and crews stayed behind, but most of the soldiers moved off towards Berlin. You could hear the fighting going on in the city all the time, day and night. The Russian tank crews did not speak to any of us. They sat in their own groups minding their own business most of the time.

Over the next few days more and more Russian soldiers came through, moving very quickly. They seemed to be in a hurry to get to Berlin. We became used to this over the following days. We stayed together and tried to maintain a routine of fetching water and finding something to eat. We walked around the edges of the fields looking in the hedgerows for birds' eggs, berries; anything we could eat. Even worms and insects were collected and boiled in water along with grass and leaves from trees; anything that might fill your stomach for a while. The Russian tank crews watched us impassively. You could not really blame them for hating us. I silently prayed that things would not turn bad and that we would survive all of this. I was in the process of squeezing the dirt out of some earthworms we had pulled from the ground. I had been shown how to prepare earthworms for eating by Tia, the BDM girl. You could not boil earthworms with dirt in them as it was toxic and could make you ill. You had to gently squeeze out the shit until you couldn't get any more out. Then you put the worms into the boiling water for a few minutes. The resulting brown-coloured broth was disgusting and tasted of nothing. The worms tended to disintegrate in the boiling water. The remaining bits were like pieces of soft jelly with no taste at all. Insects such as crickets, grasshoppers and beetles were also caught and thrown into the broth. You had to be cautious with the large black beetles. We would catch them and crush the front part to kill it. Then you would wait for five minutes. Sometimes nothing would happen and it was okay to go ahead and eat it. Sometimes, after a minute or two, a small, cotton-thin parasite would emerge from the dead beetle. I saw these on a few occasions. They looked like a piece of black cotton and wriggled out from the dead beetle. It was pretty disgusting but you had to eat. We never ate any beetles with parasites in them.

I think the Russian soldiers found our activities amusing sometimes. I remember one afternoon I was gathering bugs and things for another 'broth' as we called it. I was just about to throw some bugs we had caught into the pot when this Russian jumped down from his tank and gestured for me to stop by shaking his finger from side to side. I stopped and wondered what he wanted. He then presented a tin of what looked like some kind of meat. It had Russian print on it so I didn't know what it was. He prised off the lid with a knife then gave me the can, indicating it should be tipped into the water. I put the tin of meat in and it actually smelled very nice. The Russian raised his hand and smiled and went back to his friends. The meat he gave us tasted really nice and made a change from the tasteless rubbish we had been throwing in to the pot. Of course, there had to be a twist, as there often is with any form of kindness displayed by an enemy. The meat I had been given that afternoon was canned dog food. They fed it to the dogs that some of their units had with them. That said, even had I known what it was I would probably still have eaten it. When you are hungry you will eat anything, believe me.

A day I remember most was Monday, 30 April 1945. The Russians told us, "Hitler is dead. You lost the war." The news hit many Germans very hard. Many were convinced that Hitler was invincible. I remember years ago when he visited our street in Kreuzberg. The kindness that the man radiated towards us was something I cannot forget. I just felt numb at the news and dejected by everything around me. We had lost the war. Nobody likes to lose, do they? People ask me, "Are you still a National Socialist?" and I reply, "I was just a child at the time." Was I brainwashed beyond all compassion and understanding? No, I was not. Could I have stopped the SS from slaughtering Jews? No, I could not. It is easy for people to try and judge us and point their finger at us. Some of them do not like the fact that we survived. At the war's end we had the task of clearing up all the mess. There were displaced people who were desperately searching for their families. There were thousands of missing children. No one knew where they went or what happened to them. I was one of the lucky ones.

Tia Wittmann, who, before you ask, was not any relation to Michael [Michael Wittmann the Second World War Panzer 'Ace'], took me to live with her parents. I had no one else I could go to. The Wittmanns became like a new family to me and Tia was like a big sister and took me everywhere with her. When she married her boyfriend I was very jealous [she laughs]. They made me a bridesmaid, so I was happy with that. The Wittmanns helped me an awful lot with my education as I had missed out on so much school due to the war. I had barely ever been to school and they were concerned about my future. I later went on a secretarial course, like many young girls did back then. An old lady friend of the Wittmanns taught me how to use a typewriter and gave me a book on shorthand script writing. I worked as a secretary up until I married. We had two children. I have not let the war tarnish my life in any way, but I still miss my mother and father very much. The years that have passed since their wartime deaths have changed little. I still have moments where I look back and think about them. It saddens me what happened and I would wish it on no one. We were also very fortunate to have not lived in the east of Germany following the defeat of 1945. You are aware of everything that happened with the Cold War and the relations with Russia, so that needs no explaining. All I want is for my children and my grandchildren to be able to live their lives in peace.

Danni Foestahl, who lived in the city of Emden, has only bitter memories of the Second World War:

I can look back on it now and talk freely about it all, but for years afterwards I could not talk about it. We had to carry this label you see. The label we had to carry was the swastika and that we were all Nazi supporters who adored Adolf Hitler and cried ourselves to sleep each night that he had killed himself. I was not of that opinion at all. Embracing the initial hope that Hitler and National Socialism brought to Germany in the mid-1930s had been a terrible mistake. We soon learned that there was a sinister side to all of this. All I wanted was to be able to work and have my own space to live, making my own decisions. This was soon taken away from us, along with the promises of building a better Germany. Yes, Hitler accomplished his greater Germany, but we soon learned what a mistake it was. By that time it was too late. Totalitarian rule means opposition is brutally crushed the minute it dares to challenge those in power. Murder became the [stock in] trade of the National Socialists and they became very good at it. Some of us were aware that there were forced labour and death camps in existence. I once asked questions about the rumours [...]. They would tell you, "It's not your concern so get on with your business." They never actually denied anything. I used to think there has to be substance to the rumours. If you asked too many questions the authorities would come and pay you a visit to ask you why. It was dangerous to ask questions, so you had to just ride in the car that was going to crash. That is how I would describe Germany after 1933; a car driving along that you knew would crash at some point.

My worst memory is the dreadful air raid of 5 September 1944. Emden, such a beautiful old city, was reduced to ashes in a very short period of time. There was a school in the city with sixty-three children seeking safety in the basement below. All sixty-three children died in the bombing. They dropped 1,500 high explosives, 10,000 incendiaries and 3,000 white phosphorous bombs on the city in that raid. The white phosphorous bombs were criminal in my view. If it makes contact with your skin, white phosphorous will burn all the way through to the other side. Just a small pellet dropping into the palm of your hand will burn and fall out the other side. I saw the state of those victims who survived and they were not a pleasant sight. Many were children who had done no harm to anyone, and here they were, permanently damaged by these dreadful weapons of war. People ask me "who do you blame?" That is a question with no easy answer. We have to take a proportion of blame ourselves for allowing the Hitler regime to take power the way it did. Had the German people all stood together in opposition maybe things would have been different, but one has to bear in mind it was not that simple.

After the war we just tried to pick up the pieces, with the world calling us Nazis, calling us an evil race of people. That soon ended when the western Allies began their stand-off with Russia. They knew a bigger problem was waiting in the east. Everyone feared another war, only this time it would be the communists who would be the enemy. Communism was viewed not as a political theory back then but a disease. You could go to a doctor with some mental disorder and be told you were suffering from communism. If you expressed opinions which went against the acceptable parameters of your society, you could be condemned as suffering from communism. It was absolutely crazy, but that was the degree of western fear over communism and its attempts at spreading around the world.

I returned to my work as a hairdresser after the war. Many of the clients I used to have had been killed […]. Times were hard at first, but I worked hard. I had to repair all of the windows of my apartment, which had been smashed. My home had been looted while I had been away. Many personal documents and family photographs had been taken. Someone had urinated in what had been my bedroom. The bed was broken and the covers filthy. Pictures had been taken off the walls. It was lucky that there was nothing of much value left behind. Most of my jewellery had been taken to my parents' home, so I knew that was safe. The front door had been kicked off its hinges too, so I had to repair many things. I don't agree with the way those who won the war treated our people in 1945. The rape of women and little girls and the sodomy of young boys was not something I felt could be condoned under any circumstances. There were war crimes against the German people in this sense. But we were the evil ones, weren't we, so it was okay for them to do that to us. That was the feeling I had. Because of what the regime had done to the Jews some of us were forced to pay the price. Because they couldn't kick, beat and sodomise Hitler they did it to those they could. I felt then, and I feel now, that it was wrong.

Elizabeth Schwinn enjoyed near-celebrity status, having worked as a maid in the employment of Nazi foreign minister, Joachim von Ribbentrop:

After the war I used to get people coming up to me all the time asking me questions about the man. To be truthful, he was often bashful and boring. He seemed arrogant and selfish and not the kind of man you would want to take back home for your mother to meet. Most of those I knew who worked with him felt the same way about him. To me he was just a boss I worked for. I went and I did my job and that was it. The Allies questioned anyone who had been on the staff of prominent Nazis. What could I tell them other than what I have already said? He was just shy, boring, arrogant, selfish and full of self-importance. I was not the girl who had the task of laying out his underwear for him every evening. Nor did I have to ensure that he didn't forget to drop his false teeth in the glass of bleached water at his bedside. Of course, von Ribbentrop had his political groupies, predominantly males. He also had casual women in his life, though I think he kept those secret from his wife and family.

After the war I went to work in a laundry as I could find no work as a maid. Nobody had the money to pay you and most of the big houses had been bombed out. I went back to live with my parents for two years, which was not a bad thing. At least now it was all over I would no longer be harangued about when I would get married and start having children. Most men are worse than children, so why would I rush into marrying one? That was something I learned from the war; that most men are fucking stupid. Excuse my language, but they are. All those young, blonde-haired male tarts waltzing around in their black SS uniforms were ridiculous. The Hitler Youth, BDM, RADwf, DAF; all very articulate and regimented, but most of them would be dead by the end of May 1945.

The good thing was that the end of the Nazis meant a change of attitude evolved. We women who survived the war had proved our strength; that we did not need men to protect us and we could easily survive without them in any environment. There was no more pressure to marry or have boyfriends. We could finally think for ourselves and choose careers over children if we desired. We no longer had to follow the masses. We could be individuals again. There were many who were devastated over the death of Hitler and National Socialism. Some killed themselves because they could not deal with a Germany without Hitler. It's funny how my old boss ended up. I hadn't worked for him that long but hearing that he had been hanged made me feel for his wife and family. I felt sorry for them. Their road ahead would be a lot harder than mine.

In 1949 I had to clear some of my things from my parents' home. In one box I found a pile of cards. Most of them were from my friends but one – a white-and-gold-embossed card – was different. It bore the head of Hitler and inside it was inscribed with the words "All good wishes for Christmas and the New Year, Joachim von Ribbentrop" in blue ink. I read it through a few times before tossing it onto the log fire. I watched it shrivel up and burn. The image of Hitler's head disappearing in the flames and rapidly turning to ash was much like the memories I have of our cities when they burned, or the victims pulled from the crematoria ovens in the extermination camps. It was an episode of my history that I felt should now be laid to rest. Talking about this now is different as it is being conducted in an educational context. Education is the key to avoid making the same errors in the future. Sadly, I think Germany today is being betrayed in every sense by its own government. I often sit and watch the news and I listen to Angela Merkel speaking and I say under my breath, "You stupid, stupid woman what the hell are you doing?"

As I draw this particular volume to a close I feel that Elizabeth's words need no further explanation. Those women who have contributed to this work, with the exception of a few, led relatively trouble-free lives in the wake of the Second World War. I can only thank them for their time and for sharing some of their reminiscences which have made this volume possible. It is only a relatively brief exploration of life for the average woman on the German home front of the Second World War. An exhaustive study, however feasible it may be, would run into many volumes. That is not possible at this time. I would like to end this volume by thanking the reader for taking this journey with me. No doubt it will have its critics, but in the business of documenting Third Reich history the words of critics cannot blunt the sharpness of the memories that have made this volume possible. I would never call myself an expert; there is still much to learn and always something new waiting to be discovered. Thank you again for joining me.

Afterword

In fairytales a troll lives under every bridge and the waters that flow peacefully beneath are often possessed of vicious currents. The same principle mirrored much of that of Third Reich society, but was Germany a more aggressive nation than, say, colonial Britain? Nazism came about as a consequence of the times, borne of the unrest brought about by Germany's defeat in the First World War. Nazism was not some socio-political experiment which just happened to explode in the face of the civilized world. Nor was it an entirely new philosophy designed to appeal to a specific group of citizens. In one sense it was a departure from reasoning in a society where hope was a commodity that was unaffordable to the masses. Far from being the godly leader he so proclaimed to be, Hitler was, on reflection, little more than an immoral and politically diseased atheist, an individual hell-bent, not only on his own destruction, but that of the entire German nation. On the part of the Allies, who later had the task of liberating Western Europe from the fratricide of National Socialism, there was much to learn in the lost art of contingency planning.

As for the adoration that many of Germany's women and young girls felt towards Adolf Hitler, this amounted to nothing more than a hopeless love affair that was destined to end in disaster. Germany's females were without doubt an essential factor in the success of Hitler and the Nazi Party. Women formed a substantial part of the electorate and were partly responsible for securing his powerbase. The violence, racism and destruction, which culminated in the murder of democracy in full view of the outside world, would become the burden that many women would have to bear through the years after 1945.

Today, the general consensus of opinion of women who lived through the Third Reich was that they possessed an almost robotic, unthinking and unemotional persona. This is not entirely true and it would be unfair not to suggest otherwise. The objective of this book, therefore, was to present the reader with something a little different to the majority of publications on German social history during the days of the Third Reich. It was the women of Germany who bore the brunt of responsibilities as Germany's home front began to mobilise under the pressures brought about by the Second World War. It was they who would experience the tragedy, privations and heartache. The young girls of the *Jungmadelbund* and *Bund Deutscher Madel*, along with women well into middle age and beyond, were all called upon to help on the German home front.

There has also been the general misconception that all German girls and women were Nazis. One should remember that Nazis were not born, they had to be created and nurtured within a specific environment. One must also be reminded that not every nationalist was a fascist. Many German women continued to live their lives in as normal a context as they were able. The women of Nazi Germany were, in most respects, much like those of any other country. They lived, they loved, they laughed and they cried, the only difference being that their destinies as individuals lay in the hands of their leaders. They were required to fulfil very specific roles within the community of Nazism: obedience was ensured by the education they received as children or through their parents' affiliations with National Socialism. The sad fact is that many women had no other option than to dance with the devil.

The number of German women able to speak of their everyday wartime experiences is fast decreasing. With each passing year more succumb to old age, leaving behind any documentation they may have written, or interviews they may have given to the historian wishing to learn about their lives. One also has to understand that not all German families wish to share their own historical information. Many still view themselves as bearers of the 'crooked cross'. As an author specialising primarily in Third Reich social history, I have discovered the many pitfalls associated with such an interest. People will either praise you for the work you do or condemn you in equal measure.

I was reluctant to write something that mirrored the mundane, characterless philosophies of the 1970s history curriculum that I experienced as a child in middle school. In those days the First and Second World Wars were taboo subjects and never open for discussion in history lessons. History seemed to end with the Tudors, and I can vividly recall at just how bored I became with it all. Even then I felt it greatly disrespectful that children in school were taught nothing on the twentieth-century conflicts that shaped the world we were then living in. Challenging the history teacher on the issue would almost certainly provoke a violent response, as I found out to my cost on several occasions. By the time I left middle school, however, my history teacher, Richard Copper, and I had developed a mutual respect for one another; one based on two individuals who were polar opposites in opinion yet possessed of that same passion for history.

I felt that school, for me, was a place where it was unwise to question authority; where you were instructed what to think and denied the right to an opinion. I also recall how, even then, and despite women fighting for equality in society and the workplace, that Home Economics classes for girls were tailored towards domestic servitude. At the time it was how I imagined it might be like to live under a dictatorship.

To close, I recall the last conversation I had with Dave Garrett. We discussed many of the above topics, along with the aims of the books I had been writing, which, primarily, have focused on German women and young girls throughout the two World Wars. Although Dave had a painfully brief time left to live, the last memory he left me with was of a man not only totally at peace with the situation he was facing, but who wholeheartedly supported and encouraged what I was doing. I had intended to tell him that this next book I was preparing to write at the time would be dedicated to his memory. I couldn't find the right words to tell him in the circumstances, but I think he already knew. We also talked about his visit to the Auschwitz death camp in Poland back in 2013. For a man who had experienced much, and who had been to many places throughout his life, Auschwitz had made a deep and lasting impression on him. I would like to think that both Dave and Cy Garrett are once again reunited as father and son, and maybe enjoying a drink together while checking on the progress of Newcastle United FC and the family. This book is dedicated especially to them and all of their family, and I can only hope that I have done a job worthy of their appreciation.

Sources

No archives or other published works were consulted during the research and writing of this book. All information herein was given freely by the contributors through exclusive access to their notebooks, journals, diaries, photographs and personal letters. Various online resources, including the National Archives and Imperial War Museum in London, were consulted in order to confirm the dates of certain events that were related to me during my interviews, and to ensure that accuracy was maintained throughout the writing of this book.

Acknowledgements

I would like to thank the following for allowing me their time during the many interviews conducted during the research of this book. I would also like to extend heartfelt thanks to the German and Jewish families who allowed me unrestricted access to their personal material in the form of documents, diaries, journals, letters and photographs. This book could not have been written without them: Gertrud Hepel (was Koerg) for all material relating to the Koerg family; Roel Obermann and Alice Kaffell for all material relating to Kitka and Joachim Obermann; Adelaine Seidel; Alicia Beremont; Ursula Bomme; Giselle Durand Provost; Danni Grath (was Foestahl); Lisa Schauer; Hilde Hermann; Alessa Meissener (was Goberg); Petra Kuttner (was Oerberg); Diana Richter; Monika Graff; Gerda Rauschilde; Horst Koppfel; Ursula Topf; Hilde Eissner; Kira Runstedt; Elizabeth Schwinn; Gunther Schalk; Ingeborg Sohn.

Lyrics from 'Don't Blame Us', 'Watching the Skies' and 'Victory War is Over' appear with the kind permission of Alan 'Embo' Emms.

I would also like to extend my gratitude to the following for their unreserved support and assistance with the production of this volume: Alan Murphy, my copy-editor, who once again faced the unenviable task of preparing the basic manuscript for production. Your professionalism and patience has been a true asset. Duncan Evans, editor of *The Armourer Militaria* magazine. It is always a great privilege to have your support. Chris Warren Photography, Evesham, Worcestershire, for taking care of all my photographic needs. Lynne Powell and Ian Tustin, *The Cotswold & Vale* magazine. Claire Hopkins, history commissioning editor at Pen & Sword Books Ltd, for her faith and support throughout the writing of my books. Janet Brookes and everyone at Pen & Sword. Jody Warner, for his meticulous eye and skills with the indexing work for this volume. My partner Paula Brennan, who has had to contend with me spending many hours on the PC working on this book. The importance of having not only the right partner in your life but also the right environment in which to work as an author is a critically essential element. You do all of this and more, even when my old laptop died halfway through this project, you went out and bought me a new one, realising that I couldn't continue writing otherwise. Your love, adoration and wholehearted support is indicative of the kind, caring and loving human being you are. Lastly, I would like to thank all of my family and friends for their continued support and encouragement.

Thank you all very much and love to you all.

About the Author

Born in to a military family, Tim Heath's interest in history led him to research the air war of the Second World War, focussing on the German Luftwaffe and writing extensively for *The Armourer* Magazine. During the course of his research he has worked closely with the German War Graves Commission at Kassel, Germany, and met with German families and veterans alike. Following the successful debut of *Hitler's Girls, Hitler's Housewives* will be Tim's fifth book to contribute to this overlooked part of an otherwise heavily scrutinised period of history.

Tim lives near the old market town of Evesham, Worcestershire with his partner Paula.

Index